Life's Losses

LIVING THROUGH GRIEF, BEREAVEMENT AND SUDDEN CHANGE

Life's Losses

LIVING THROUGH GRIEF,
BEREAVEMENT AND
SUDDEN CHANGE

Betty Jane Wylie

MACMILLAN CANADA
TORONTO

Canadian Cataloguing in Publication Data

Wylie, Betty Jane, 1931-
    Life's losses : living through grief,
    bereavement and sudden change

Includes index.

ISBN 0-7715-7377-4

1. Loss (Psychology).   2. Bereavement – Psychological aspects.   3. Grief.   I. Title.

BF575.G7W85 1996   155.9'37   C95-932621-9

1 2 3 4 5 / 00 99 98 97 96

Cover design by Campbell Sheffield Design Inc.

Macmillan Canada wishes to thank the Canada Council and the Ontario Ministry of Culture and Communications for supporting its publishing program.

Macmillan Canada
A Division of Canada Publishing Corporation
Toronto, Ontario, Canada

Printed in Canada

To Tillie Olsen, who knows

Preface

IF YOU THINK YOU CAN'T HANDLE GRIEF, READ THIS AND learn how much you already know. But this is not a how-to book; there are no step-by-step instructions to help you out of the morass of fear or doubt or pain you find yourself in. And it's not Mother Wylie telling you how to cope. It's just me, after all, a communicative human being, possibly your friend, attempting to analyze some of the reasons for, and the meaning of, the many and continuous losses we all meet – not on the road less travelled but on the road no one can avoid. I'm not a tour guide, just a talkative tourist.

Life's Losses is a generic book about grief, all kinds of grief, the grief we feel in varying and increasing degrees throughout our lives as we encounter life's losses. Surveying them like that, you'd think you might be depressed by them. Not so. Grieving is an ongoing creative process.

Somewhere along the way I have learned to be rueful about loss and sensitive to pain without becoming either callous or overwhelmed. Gratitude, acceptance and contentment are possible. I wouldn't go quite so far as to call my attitude the Joy of Grieving but is has been done: the poet Kahlil Gibran described joy as sorrow unmasked. I have simply learned to cherish the precious moments and to allow the bad times to roll when they must. I just keep on counting my blessings. You can too.

Contents

Acknowledgments

A book like this doesn't get written without a lot of help. First, I would like to thank all the people who wrote to me of their discoveries on this hard path — Joyce Beaton, Elaine Gort, Vernie Juras, Donalda MacKenzie, Olive Thiesenhausen, and Sharon Thorpe, to name a few, but there are others who wish to be nameless. I have scattered their comments and ideas and revelations among my own.

My long-time friend Judy Bager and Rev. Clifford Elliott helped me with special information I didn't have. My friend and temp help Kathleen Flaherty made sense of the copyright permissions and pulled me out of a sea of paper. Then there's Michelle Morra, the research assistant lent to me for a month by Sheridan College — such an assignment for a young woman, to read sad tales of death and disaster, and take notes! And Jennifer Glossop, my editor, is always there, thank heaven — always Jennifer: so harsh and sympathetic, so demanding and responsive. Thank you.

Care has been taken to trace ownership of copyright material contained in this book. I will gladly receive any information that will enable me to rectify any reference or credit line in subsequent editions. Grateful acknowledgment is made for permission to quote from materials listed below:

The Denial of Death by Ernest Becker. Copyright © 1973 by The Free Press. Reprinted by permission of The Free Press, a division of Macmillan Publishing Co., Inc.

Twelve Weeks in Spring by June Callwood. Copyright © June Callwood, 1986. Toronto: Lester & Orpen Dennys Limited. Reprinted with permission of the author.

Widower by Scott Campbell and Phyllis Silverman, Ph.D. Copyright © 1987 by Scott Campbell. Reprinted by permission of the publisher, Prentice Hall Press, a division of Simon & Schuster, New York, N.Y.

A Day at a Time, edited by Margo Culley. Copyright © 1985 by The Feminist Press. Reprinted by permission of The Feminist Press, New York.

When Things Get Back to Normal by M. T. Dohaney. Copyright © 1989 M. T. Dohaney. Reprinted by permission of Pottersfield Press, Porter's Lake, Nova Scotia.

In a Different Voice by Carol Gilligan. Copyright © 1982 by Carol Gilligan. Reprinted by permission of Harvard University Press, Cambridge, Mass.

Prayer Before an Abortion by Linda Griffiths from *The Darling Family*. Copyright © 1989 by Linda Griffiths. Published in *Prairie Journal of Canadian Literature*, No. 12, 1989–90. Reprinted by permission of the author.

Dr. Earl A. Grollman, from a speech delivered to the Bereaved Families of Ontario, Ottawa chapter, May 1990. Reprinted by permission of Dr. Grollman.

Death: The Final Stage of Growth by Elisabeth Kübler-Ross. Copyright © 1975 by Elisabeth Kübler-Ross. Reprinted by permission of Simon & Schuster.

Toward a New Psychology of Women by Jean Baker Miller. Copyright © 1976, 1986 by Jean Baker Miller. Reprinted by permission of Beacon Press, Boston, Mass.

ACKNOWLEDGMENTS

Friend of My Youth by Alice Munro. Copyright © 1990 by Alice Munro. Used by permission of the Canadian Publishers, McClelland and Stewart, Toronto.

The Healing Brain by Robert Ornstein & David Sobel. Copyright © 1987 by The Institute for the Study of Human Knowledge. Reprinted by permission of Simon & Schuster.

Tissue by Louise Page. Copyright © 1982 by Louise Page. From *Plays by Women*, volume one. ed. by Micheline Wandor, Methuen Drama, London. Reprinted by permission of Methuen Drama, London.

The Road Less Traveled by M. Scott Peck. Copyright © 1978 by M. Scott Peck. Reprinted by permission of Simon & Schuster.

No Longer Than a Sigh by Anne Philipe. Copyright © 1964 by Rene Julliard, Paris. Reprinted with permission of Atheneum Publishers, an imprint of Macmillan Publishing Company, from *No Longer Than a Sigh* by Anne Philipe, translated by Cornelia Schaeffer.

Midstream by Le Anne Schreiber. Copyright © 1990 by Le Anne Schreiber. Reprinted by permission of Viking, Penguin.

"Living With Loss, Dreaming of Lace" by Mimi Schwartz. Copyright © 1990. Reprinted by permission of *Lear's* magazine from the October 1990 issue.

Certificate in Escrow by Steve Stanton. Copyright © 1989 by Steve Stanton. Published in *Prairie Journal of Canadian Literature*, No. 12, 1989–90. Reprinted by permission of the author.

Do Not Go Gentle into That Good Night by Dylan Thomas from *The Poems* (J.M. Dent & Sons, 1971). Copyright © 1937 by the Trustees for the Copyrights of Dylan Thomas. Reprinted by permission of David Higham Associates Limited.

Future Shock by Alvin Toffler. Copyright © 1970 by Alvin Toffler. Reprinted by permission of Random House, Inc.

Addiction to Perfection by Marion Woodman. Copyright © 1982 by Marion Woodman. Reprinted by permission of Inner City Books, Toronto.

Coping: A Survival Manual for Women Alone by Martha Yates. Copyright © 1976 by Prentice-Hall, Inc. Reprinted by permission of the publisher, Prentice Hall, a division of Simon & Schuster, Englewood Cliffs, New Jersey.

The Hour of Our Death by Philippe Ariès. Copyright © 1981 by Alfred A. Knopf, Inc. Alfred A. Knopf, New York. Reprinted by permission.

The Faber Book of Diaries, edited by Simon Brett. Copyright © Simon Brett 1987. Faber & Faber, London. Reprinted by permission.

Attachment by John Bowlby. Basic Books, Tavistock Institute, England.

A Bridge For Passing by Pearl Buck. Copyright © 1961, 1962 by Pearl S. Buck. Harper & Row, New York.

The Mermaid and the Minotaur by Dorothy Dinnerstein. Copyright © 1976 by Dorothy Dinnerstein. Harper Colophon Books, New York.

Just As You Are by Virginia Sheeley Dustin. *Good Housekeeping*, March 1989.

Man's Search for Meaning by Viktor E. Frankl. Copyright © 1959, 1962 by Viktor E. Frankl. Beacon Press, Boston.

The Prophet by Kahlil Gibran. Copyright © 1923 by Kahlil Gibran, renewal copyright 1951 by Administrators C.T.A. of Kahlil Gibran Estate and Mary G. Gibran. Alfred A. Knopf, New York. Reprinted by permission.

Death Be Not Proud by John Gunther. Copyright © 1949 by John Gunther. Harper & Row, New York.

The Day After Death by Linda Hartman from Mary Jane Moffatt (ed.) *In the Midst of Winter*. © 1982 by Linda Hartman.

Holmes and Raye *Journal of Psychosomatic Research*, Vol. 11, 1967.

Brand by Henrik Ibsen, translated by F. E. Garrett. J.M. Dent & Son, London.

Impro by Keith Johnstone. Copyright © Keith Johnstone 1979. Faber & Faber, London.

Loss and Change by Peter Marris. Copyright © 1974 by the Institute of Community Studies. Anchor Books, Doubleday, Garden City, New York.

Dirge Without Music by Edna St. Vincent Millay. Copyright © 1928, 1955 by Edna St. Vincent Millay. Elizabeth Barnett, Literary Executor.

A Canticle for Liebowitz by Walter M. Miller. Copyright © 1959 by Walter M. Miller, Jr. Bantam Books, New York.

So Long, See You Tomorrow by William Maxwell. Copyright © 1979 by William Maxwell. Originally appeared in *The New Yorker*. Reprinted by permission of Alfred A. Knopf.

Borrowed Time by Paul Monette. Copyright © 1988 Paul Monette. Avon Books, New York.

Death and the Family by Lily Pincus. Copyright © 1974 by Lily Pincus. Vintage Books, Random House, New York.

Some Men Are More Perfect Than Others by Merle Shain. Copyright © 1973 by Merle Shain. Bantam Books, Toronto.

The Doctor's Dilemma by George Bernard Shaw. Little Brown & Co.

The Making of the Modern Family by Edward Shorter. Copyright © 1977 by Edward Shorter. Copyright © 1975 by Basic Books, Inc. Basic Books, Harper & Row, New York.

Nobody Here But Us Chickens by Elizabeth Smart. From *A Bonus*, published by Polytantric Press, London.

A Book About My Mother by Toby Talbot. Copyright © 1980 by Toby Talbot. Farrar, Straus and Giroux, New York.

Words for a Deaf Daughter by Paul West. New York: Harper & Row, 1970.

A Room of One's Own by Virginia Woolf. Copyright © Quentin Bell and Angelica Garnett, 1928. Harcourt Brace Jovanovich, New York.

Lines of poetry not otherwise attributed in the text are from Betty Jane Wylie, *Something Might Happen* (Windsor, Black Moss Press, 1989).

Introduction

DEATH IS IMPLICIT IN EVERY LIVING ORGANISM ON THIS planet. We begin to die the moment we draw first breath. One might say we are goal-oriented, aimed at death, from our first stumbling steps. Throughout our lives we encounter metaphors for death: the plans abandoned, hopes dashed, efforts frustrated, ambitions thwarted, aspirations disappointed, promises broken, love denied. All the losses, great and small, are like a rehearsal, training us for the eventual loss of our own life.

Wisdom is not won without pain. We must believe that out of pain will come wisdom and understanding. We cling tenaciously to that belief against apparent reality, to preserve hope. No one ever said it is easy; few have said that it is necessary. It is. We die anyway, so we might as well live as creatively as we can. We do so by grieving, by absorbing and assimilating loss and growing with it, not in spite of it but because of it.

Grieving can be a creative process.

When loss comes, the effect is staggering. When it comes, it seems impossible to surmount. The burden is unbearable but it must be borne; the suffering is unendurable but must be endured. Fate is unavoidable in spite of all our efforts to avoid, even ignore it. The only comfort is that one finds oneself briefly in the eye of the storm — spurious comfort, too short, too precarious. One must eventually work through the maelstrom. The worst of the buffeting is almost over by the time one develops sufficient strength to endure it. One learns to grasp and use the tools of survival.

What tools? Until we need them, we are scarcely aware of them. Only when we have reached wit's and tether's end, having tried everything, do we finally turn to these simple concepts. Consider these tools:

1. Our role

We must consider carefully our role in life — whoever we are. We are human: female, male, wife, mother, husband, father, someone's child, someone's parent, someone's employee or employer, someone's friend. None of the above? Human, anyway. One thing we must always refuse to be, or to play, is victim. That is not a role, that is a perception. We must try to define our role, not by what we do but by what we are. Our clear comprehension of self is one of the tools of survival.

2. Our assignment

Everyone has a job to do. We are here for a reason. The reason may be obscure to us, and it may be a very small one in the history of the world, but the fact of our existence is reason enough. No one can be replaced and no one will be repeated. We must ask, then, before we do anything rash, if we have finished our task.

3. Suffering

Suffering is the most powerful tool. By our role and our assignment we have already learned what kind of suffering we're in for. When the struggle for basic physical survival, that is, for shelter and food and relative safety, has been (more or less) met, then begins the psychological battle. Our ability to suffer is the key that will help us unlock the door to understanding.

4. Weakness

Remember the rigid, mighty oak tree that cracked and snapped in the storm while the pliant, frail reed bent and survived? Every time one of us survives, we gain a kind of supple, yielding strength. "Roll with the punches," goes the saying. Anyone who has suffered a muscle spasm knows that resistance makes it worse. In order to gain relief, one must allow the spasm to run its course, work through the aching muscles. Afterwards, the vivid memory of pain remains, but so also does the sure knowledge of survival.

5. Our burden
Psychiatrist Viktor Frankl points out that, "if architects want to strengthen a decrepit arch, they *increase* the load which is laid upon it, for thereby the parts are joined more firmly together." There is an old saying: "The same flame that melts butter tempers steel." The idea is that the stress, the flame, the pain — in short, the burden — is in itself the source of strength. The very act of bearing it is an indication of surviving it.

6. Grace
Workers in the Third World report a strange phenomenon manifest among the people they work with and try to help. Sick, starving, suffering human beings act less aggressively than might be expected. Instead, they exhibit dignity, express compassion for others, and show themselves capable of incredible acts of selflessness. One of the phrases given to me by a friend when I was suffering most was this: guts and grace. "You will survive, lady," he said, "because you have guts and grace." A warning: grace is a spiritual gift. We're not going to be able to talk about survival without dealing with the spiritual. I'll be gentle.

7. Guts
He said it, I didn't — guts (and grace). Guts: backbone, pluck, valor, mettle, grit, nerve, spunk, courage. Even people who think they don't have any have guts. Some of the quiet, brave ones don't recognize their own courage, the ones who rise each day to chronic physical pain but who still manage to do their work and even smile occasionally, the lonely ones who keep themselves busy, the overworked ones who find time for others (but not enough for themselves), the threatened ones (financially, mentally, spiritually) who nevertheless keep trying to find practical solutions to their problems. Examples abound, and I will cite many of them.

8. Choice

One cannot choose what happens. Up to a point, perhaps, but there are immutable laws one cannot change. For example, what goes up must come down. It's called gravity: a body that falls out of a tree will probably be hurt. Occasionally one reads about someone who survives a plunge from an apartment balcony or a plane, but that's why it's news — it's a fluke. There is still such a thing as luck, but we can't count on it. Here's another one: when an immovable object meets an irresistible force, something has to give: again if it's a body in the way of a car, the body gets killed, usually. Germs and viruses cause diseases, and if they're strong enough and the body is sick enough, the body dies. There are more cures now, since the miracle drugs were discovered, but we keep running out of miracles. The survival tool here, however, is not inherent in the event, the accident, or the disease. It lies in one's attitude to what has happened. This area is the only one in which there is a choice. How we choose to look at what has happened colors the event. Is the glass half-empty, half-full, or "just half," as one sick person said to me recently. Frankl says this is "the last of human freedoms: the ability to choose one's attitude in a given set of circumstances." The choice is ours.

Thus, there are at least eight tools for survival. Some of them may never have been considered as tools; others we are simply not aware of possessing. All of them will prove, have proved, useful. There are no easy answers or pat solutions to the problems of life and death. It's harder to lose than to be lost. Clutching at straws never did much good for anyone, least of all the person who watches both straw and clutcher disappear into the vortex. If we gather our tools — ahead of time would be preferable, but I'm probably asking too much — and use them well, then we can not only survive life's losses but also grow with them. The last tool, choice, is an act of creation.

Grieving can be a creative process.

With this in mind, I propose to examine grief from a long-term, lifetime view. As we all anticipate longer lives, so we all confront death and loss more frequently. The very fact of our living so long makes this sad fact inevitable. Aging becomes a loss in itself, accompanied by the deterioration of physical and sometimes mental capacities. Some people live long enough to suffer the death of an adult child, or to become both caregiver and prisoner of a spouse with a lingering disease. Younger people can lose a child not only through miscarriage, stillbirth, the agonizing choice of abortion, or cancer (one of the leading causes of the death of children), but also through abduction, murder, or suicide. The death of a relationship through separation or divorce can be just as devastating as the physical death of a loved one. No one living is exempt from death or loss. Ultimately, we are all survivors, and victims, but we must never think of ourselves as victims.

We who have lived so long have not done so without learning something along the way. Sharing sorrow helps us come to terms with our own; pooling wisdom enables us to acquire more. Traveling together on this hard road equips us to find a new path through pain. In searching for the self we think we have lost, we may also find a new creative role.

I

LOSS

Loss is permanent and leaves scars.
Scars are private, but their causes and effects are public.

1. A Definition of Loss

Losing is the price we pay for living.
— JUDITH VIORST

LOSS IS A CONSTANT. LOSS IS A FACT OF LIFE, AND PERHAPS the only constant — from birth: loss of the protection of the womb, loss of mother's milk (some sooner than later); through childhood: loss of baby teeth, loss of friends, of innocence; to maturity: loss of home, of parents, of lover, companion, spouse (if not now, then later), of expectations; to old age: loss of job, of role, of lifestyle, independence, self, ending up, as Shakespeare described, "sans teeth, sans eyes, sans taste, sans everything." Painful aberrations skew the familiar pattern: a child must endure the loss of one or both parents through divorce or death (or neglect, abuse, or alcoholism), a parent staggers with the loss of a child through disease, accident, drugs, disappearance, suicide, murder.

All change in life results from losses, even seemingly trivial ones. One set of dependencies is forfeited for the next. Life challenges us with a series of steps as in the old children's game — Giant, Baby, Scissor, Side, and sometimes Back — but moves on inexorably. One encounters turns, detours, obstacles, and steep grades along the way, and is delayed, staggered, slowed, stopped. Sometimes a rest period is granted, a breathing space, a plateau before the next assault, but it never lasts. "Life," as Carl Jung said, "behaves as if it goes on," and it does, sometimes too quickly.

At whatever speed, changes occur for everyone and changes always involve loss. Even what is perceived as gain is accompanied by loss. Falling in love, and being loved in return, means giving up part of one's self to the loved one, who becomes a hostage to fate, one to whom something is owed. A new job means leaving the old one and sometimes a home and friends if the job entails moving to another place. A new baby splits one forever, as one draws breath and responsibility for two (or more). Adventure can mean abandonment, arrival can mean estrangement, a new beginning always means an earlier termination.

We lose our toys, our homes, our purpose, our goals, our future. We lose our resilience, adaptability, vigor, stamina; we lose our parents, children, companions; eventually we all lose life, for no one is exempt from death, the ultimate loss.

But one could substitute another word for loss: gain. As we move on, leaving a trail of things, people, and memories behind us, we gain something else: new horizons, new perspectives, a new focus, new strength. This is never easy. This is no Pollyanna Glad Game, no simplistic attempt to look on the bright side. This is a tough, relentless pursuit of fulfilment. We lose markers, we gain ground; we lose tools, we gain strength; we lose tokens, we gain creation.

> To every thing there is a season, and a time to every purpose under the heaven. . . . A time to get, and a time to lose; a time to keep, and a time to cast away.
> — ECCLESIASTES 3: 1–6

Every loss is accompanied by a gain. What I propose to prove is that every loss of self is a Giant Step forward, a creative leap toward a new self. What we are after is that shining new self — the one that others find hard to recognize, disguised as it is by amputation and scars, by frailty and wrinkles, by blurred hesitancy and blinding pain. The core can be strong and shiny and new, transcending life's blows and death's seeming triumph.

John Bowlby wrote three volumes about separation and loss, beginning with the long-lasting effects on children of early separation resulting from death or other trauma. Bowlby notes that the behavior in very young people is strikingly similar to that in adults. He says that there is a tendency "to under-estimate how intensely distressing and disabling loss is," and notes how long such distress and disablement last. Bereaved families tend to make light of childhood losses, considering them to be short-lived and not as searing as they are for the older members. Not so. We will discuss grief in children later, in connection with the death of a parent or a sibling, but consider for a moment other losses children suffer.

My older daughter was racked with sobs one night as I went to tuck her in. I thought at the very least that my quivering little four-year-old must have cut herself to the quick. She *was* hurt to the quick but her wound didn't bleed. "I've lost Karen," she said, her voice quavering. Five-year-old Karen had started kindergarten and declared that she wasn't going to bother with babies like Liz any more. I thought of that recently when I lost a friend I'd had since I was eight years old. Pain knifed into my stomach when I received a Christmas present I had sent her, returned unopened. Rejection, guilt for one's own responsibility, anger, and then simple pain (not so simple) combine to make the loss of a friend at any age hurt like hell. Children aren't the only ones to experience these emotions, but let's not forget that children do suffer them.

These days, with about one-third of the population moving house every year, most children endure the loss of friends and familiar surroundings through geographical separation. For a very young child, the move need not even be out of town; even a move to a different neighborhood makes a difference to someone who has to rely on grownups for transportation. Coupled with a transfer to a new school, with new teachers, and strangers in the playground, a move at any age can be difficult. When the move has been caused by a death or a divorce in the family, it can be traumatic.

The loss of a pet often presents a child's first encounter with death and can be painful, especially if the child is a loner and the pet was a favorite companion. In contrast, an apparent gain — to everyone else — of a new brother or sister can threaten a child grievously. A new baby automatically changes one's position in the family, even if one is no longer lonely and only. Divided parental attention means less to each individual child, and cuddly new babies are time-consuming and cuter than the older, green-eyed sibling. The death of a sibling is even worse. The child seems to have lost two parents as well. Preoccupied as the adults are with their own loss, they sometimes forget or trivialize the needs of their other child/children for whom life, which once seemed safe and predictable, will never be the same again.

It never is. Every loss is based on change, and every change is irrevocable. No one can ever recover yesterday. Most changes destroy the future as well, and constitute another kind of loss. In his 1970 book, *Future Shock*, Alvin Toffler warns that there are limits to our adaptability, and he offers some suggestions for coping with change and the shock of tomorrow. He encourages us to cultivate habits we can keep, even in a shifting society and with changing lifestyles. Habit and ritual and something like fidelity to a few close friends (and spouses and children) provide some semblance of stability in a changing world. The secret, Toffler suggests, is not to suppress change, but to manage it.

By now, everyone probably knows about Thomas Holmes and Richard Rahe and the stress score, but I'll include it as a memory refresher.

Social Readjustment Rating Scale

Note that the majority of these life changes involve loss of some kind.

LIFE EVENT	LIFE CHANGE UNIT VALUE
Death of spouse	100
Divorce	73
Marital separation	65
Jail term	63
Death of close family member	63
Personal injury or illness	53
Marriage	50
Fired at work	47
Marital reconciliation	45
Retirement	45
Change in family health	44
Pregnancy	40
Sex difficulties	39
Gain of new family member	39
Business readjustment	39

Social Readjustment Rating Scale (continued)

LIFE EVENT	LIFE CHANGE UNIT VALUE
Change in financial state	38
Death of close friend	37
Change to different line of work	36
Arguments with spouse	35
Mortgage	31
Foreclosure of mortgage or loan	30
Change in job responsibilities	29
Son or daughter leaving home	29
Trouble with in-laws	29
Major personal achievement	28
Mate begins or stops work	26
Begin or end school	26
Change in living conditions	25
Revision of personal habits	24
Trouble with boss	23
Change in work conditions	20
Change in residence	20
Change in schools	20
Change in recreation	19
Change in church activities	19
Change in social activities	18
Loan	17
Change in sleeping habits	16
Change in family get-togethers	15
Change in eating habits	15
Vacation	13
Christmas	12
Minor violations of the law	11

The Schedule of Recent Experience (SRE) and the Social Readjustment Rating Scale (SRRS), first proposed in 1967, rate the stress involved in life events and assign them a score, beginning with the highest, 100, for the death of a spouse down to the lowest, 11, for a traffic violation. (Some psychologists have suggested that the divorce score of 73 should be interchanged with the score for death as being more stressful.) The reason for keeping such a score is to evaluate the stress an individual is under and to attempt to prevent it from becoming health-threatening. Too high a score within a twelve-month period, it has been proved, can result in serious illness, including a heart attack or a stroke. Thus it's advisable to limit the stress load, or if such is not possible, then to control and manage it. Basically, stress management means the management of change. We are advised not to make too many moves or sudden changes in life if we can help it. That is why widows (and new mothers) are told not to move within the first year of their Life Event, why raw divorcees shouldn't change jobs, and why recent widowers and divorced men should run the other way rather than jump into an affair too soon. Enough is enough, and too much can be a killer.

Stress is a popular subject these days, and experts offer advice ranging from common sense to radical treatment to help people cope with it. Stress, however, is merely a symptom, albeit serious, of a deeper, more basic problem. Anger has been cited as the cause of stress, the anger caused by the gap between eager expectations and grim reality. These expectations may be focused on other people, on a career, on some external source of looked-for happiness, or they may be turned inward, demanding high performance levels and impeccable behavior from oneself. Either way, no one ever lives up to expectations. This gap causes anger, which in turn causes stress. If we look deeper, we can see that change is the trigger, loss the cause, and anger and stress merely (!) the symptoms. When people undergo a change, they lose their continuity. Life's moving parts become incomprehensible, patterns shift, meaning skews, confidence disintegrates. One must wrestle with loss in much the same way one copes with grief, by a process of psychological adjustment. Easier said than done.

We are all conservative when it comes to change. Even the most radical thinkers would prefer life to go on as expected. The will to restore the past (sometimes called tradition) exerts a strong influence in any human being, from child to adult. "Why can't things go on as they were?" we plead. "I liked my life the way it was" — even, sometimes, when life as it was, was hell.

Resistance to change is itself a way of life. We are all creatures of habit, doing things the way they should be done. We expect to follow the "rules" and expect others to do so as well: to behave "normally," conform to accepted patterns, obey the precepts of society and follow its code of behavior and principles. In so doing, we fool ourselves into thinking that life is manageable, predictable, and maybe even meaningful. That's how most of us survive, until something pulls the familiar carpet out from under our feet. That's when we stiffen as we stumble, freeze as we fall, and scream as the abyss of the unknown opens beneath us. Change threatens our stability, and loss undermines our hold on both sanity and life.

Our personal encounters with death are devastating; they profoundly affect our emotions and our behavior. An individual assessment, therefore, a recap of one's own experiences, and a pulse-taking, would be useful for anyone facing grief. It is only in one's own history that the clues to present behavior and future recovery may be found. I offer a glimpse of one person's private history, my own particular confrontations with death, and (briefly) what I have learned, in the hope that such an account will stimulate private memories and personal clues to survival in my readers.

2. A Private History of Death

O, death, where is thy sting? O grave, where is thy victory?
— I CORINTHIANS 15:55

AS I CAST MY MEMORY BACK TO CATCH WHAT I CAN OF MY early and later impressions of death, I hope that these recollections may trigger memories in my readers. Children have a strange, pragmatic understanding of life and death, a kind of stoic, bewildered acceptance. There is so much that is strange; all a very young child can do is file away incidents and unrelated facts. Later it may be possible to make some sort of synthesis.

I can remember early on (age four?) a goldfish jumping out of the bowl while its water was being changed, splashing into the toilet bowl, and being flushed away. It wasn't dead, just gone. Like the wolf in *Little Red Ridinghood*. Grandma isn't dead, not killed by the wolf, just in his stomach; later, in some versions of the story, she comes out intact, unchewed.

I can also remember staging a couple of funerals: one for a wounded bird my brother and I had tried to save, one for a pet white mouse. For the mouse we coaxed our mother to empty a box of Eddy wooden matches for us to use as a coffin. We were more intent on the trappings than on the event, and in that I think we shared a traditional attitude.

One of my favorite stories involves a Winnipeg friend who tried to persuade her kids to give their dead mouse a decent burial in the garbage can rather than dig a grave in six feet of snow in the back yard.

"Think of the poor mouse in the cold ground," my friend said, seeing herself struggling in that deep snow. "Think how much cozier it will be in a nice warm garbage can," she said.

"Mother!" said her daughter, in that withering tone only daughters achieve. "The mouse is dead. The funeral is for us."

People—even children whom we seem to leave out when it comes to dealing with death these days—know instinctively what funerals are for. I dwell on this because I want to emphasize the gap between public and private thinking. The community at large can be very stupid, even insensitive, but most individuals have a gut instinct about what they're doing and what's best for them, if only we would let them get on with it. They know, at least, that funerals are for the living. Funerals provide the opportunity for relatives and friends to pay their respects, drop off some flowers or a donation or a casserole, and go on with what they were doing. Thanks to undertakers, a tiny amount of ritual still remains attached to the day itself and to the mechanics of disposing of the body.

I saw my first dead body when I was six or seven. My father was a doctor in an age when doctors made house calls and worked on Sundays. He liked to have company in the car as he made his rounds, and his family liked the opportunity to visit with him while he drove. Sometimes, however, the interval between chats was tedious and, if his call took too long on a winter day, cold. Parked outside what I didn't know was a funeral home, I was forced by the cold into the quiet building to seek warmth and my father. The waiting room was empty; I had a choice of doors. I opened one and found a large, austere room, empty save for one person lying in a silk-lined box more like a large, padded crib than a bed. He was very white and very very still and I knew awe, though I didn't know the word. I left the building and went back to the cold car, not now as cold as that room seemed. I told my father what I had done, what I had seen, and he must have explained death to me in a way I could accept because I don't remember having had any inordinate fear or nightmares. I never forgot that stillness, not at all like sleep, and I even remember the man's name after all these years.

About a year after that, I saw the body of the headmistress of the private convent school I attended. (I wasn't Catholic, just smart and needing attention.) Mother Superior's body had to be shipped back to the convent cemetery in Montreal. Following a funeral service in the school's tiny chapel, we — the pupils and the staff, all nuns — accompanied the coffin to the train station to see her off. That was the beginning of my detachment, the awareness of a separation of heart from head. I found myself *observing* the scene, as if I were taking notes. We stood on the platform, trapped by the railway's schedule, and I remember the steam hissing out of the train and the white cloud hanging there like a wraith in the below-zero cold — probably my first experience of pathetic fallacy, though, of course, I didn't know the term. I remember one girl, older than me, running forward and breaking a yellow rose off the spray on top of the coffin, kissing it and weeping, clutching her memento as a prize. I couldn't do that, though I loved Mother Superior. We shared the same birthday, and each year she gave me one of her gifts, a doll's dress made for her by one of the children in Junior School.

I had already said goodbye to her. Each of us had been allowed into the chapel before the service for a few moments alone with our surrogate mother. So I was alone with a dead body for the second time in my life (eight years old by this time). She/it was beautiful, very white and very still. No still life was ever as still as death. I learned that early. People who say that the deceased looks to be asleep are lying or deceiving themselves. There's a lot of deception flying around the dead and dying. We'll encounter more as we go along.

I didn't see another dead person until I was in my teens. My father's father had died somewhere in there, but I had been told nothing about it until I was taken to visit Grandma in her new apartment and wondered aloud where Grandpa would sleep. He had gone away on a long trip, I was told, and wasn't coming back. Thus were children excluded from death in my childhood, or at least in my family. I learned only two pieces of information connected with my grandfather's death, long after the fact.

He had dropped dead (heart) after his morning shave. My father told me that, when the body was being prepared for the funeral, the face had to be shaved again, thus informing me that hair continues to grow after death. The other fact turned out to be inaccurate as well. My father always described his own future death as paralleling his father's. "When I have my heart attack and die," he'd say, and I believed him, so much so that, when he did have his heart attack, for days no one could convince me that he wasn't dying. We were both astonished when he survived and lived to die of cancer ten years later.

When I was sixteen and a member of a college fraternity (our sorority called itself a fraternity out of misguided, inaccurate feminism), one of our sisters died suddenly, over a weekend, from a case of galloping poliomyelitis. Her funeral was a twentieth-century example of group mourning; her fraternity sisters attended en masse, each of us wearing our membership pin and dissolving when we saw the deceased's pinned on her sweater; she, dressed in her coffin as if going off to a morning class as soon as the funeral was over. One always remembers the details.

Again an odd memory: hyper (we didn't use that word in those days) and distraught, I went straight from the funeral to a mass I.Q. test for all second-year students. Grapevine reports later hinted that I scored very well in that test, though no one ever told me so officially. I still remember my mind detaching itself from my funeral-wrought emotions, putting me in some sort of free-wheeling overdrive, remote and smoothly functioning. When the bell rang to signify the end of the test, I jumped, startled to be thus restored to my body and real time. So, I remember this, too, as one of the byproducts of heightened emotion: detachment, efficiency, and a sense of unreality.

One year later another of our fraternity sisters died, of Hodgkin's disease; it took her about three months and must have emaciated her, because this time the coffin was closed — or perhaps the family didn't want to share her. We learned of the death from our Dean of Women, who called four of us out of our classes and lent us her car (an unprecedented favor) so we could go off campus and have coffee and talk. I was seventeen with a recent driver's license (what can that dear woman have been thinking of?). Following a February thaw and a quick-freeze, Winnipeg streets were icy, and my braking reflex, too swift at a stop, spun us twice and into snow piled deep enough to bumper the car clear of a telephone pole. That near-miss slowed me down at the time, but it also taught me, on cool recall, something about hair-trigger nerves and the tension accompanying a Life Event.

Our little sorority was considered jinxed and had trouble recruiting new members the next year. Death does this, labels as pariahs and outcasts those too closely associated with it. Come away, come away, come away, death. The skull behind the mask still grins hideously, try as we may to pretend it isn't there.

Then my family started dying, not immediate members, but getting closer. It's a war of nerves, the one between life and death; little by little, death picks off the ones around the central figure, getting closer all the time. The closest thus far was my maternal grandmother. The funeral service took place in Gimli, where my grandparents had lived and raised their children after they emigrated from Iceland. I remember my grandfather asking everyone if they had seen my grandmother in her coffin. "Did you see her?" he kept asking, "Did you see her lying in there? Just like a young girl she looked, so lovely, just the way she looked on her wedding day." I learned something about the eyes of love that day. My other memory is of the church bell; it was so cold out that each ring was followed by a heavy *thunk* as the frozen metal protested. Again, the watcher, the listener in me was paying attention to details I could use. For what?

I was stricken by the death of a favorite dog while I was still at university, and mocked for my emotion. Sandy was the only animal I ever cried over. I still remember my reaction and thus can sympathize with others who are so moved by the loss of a pet. Sandy was the companion of my lonely adolescence; I needed him. Animals are sometimes better than people, and often more available to provide silent comfort, physical contact and warmth, something to cling to. It has been medically proved now that more heart-attack victims with pets recover, and more swiftly, than those without. The grief following the death of a pet can be so real that, just as with departed human beings, the bereaved can hear the dog scratching at the door, pushing its bowl in the kitchen, snoring in its sleep. In fact, these delusions, produced by projection from the grieving one's mind, indicate that similar projections (sight, more usually sound) of a departed human being come from the projector's mind and not from the Hereafter — unless there really is a Doggy Heaven.

I continue with my personal roster of death. There were a few suicides along the way: a very serious young man with whom I had been friends several years earlier, the brother of a friend, my cousin's brother-in-law. These were strange deaths; I had no comprehension of them, intellectual or emotional. Amazingly, although all my male relatives (and one female one) had been in the Second World War, none of them had died. Friends had lost brothers and fathers; I was unscathed.

My husband had experienced a number of deaths in his family at an early age. Three of his mother's stalwart brothers — that is, all his uncles except the youngest, who lived in England — and one young aunt, as well as his maternal grandmother, died during Bill's childhood and adolescence. When Bill was nine, his father died in a car crash. He fell asleep at the wheel en route to the family on vacation at a lake — or was it a heart attack? Bill's grandfather and maiden aunt then moved in with Bill's family, and the old man became a surrogate father. Thus, his death, five years later, hit the boy hard.

It's not as if these brushes with death provide instruction, some kind of preliminary training for the main event, hardening and preparing one for pain. Grief doesn't work like that. Too much horror does; it builds a protective shell and hardens it. Psychologists worry now that too many violent deaths on television desensitize people, adults as well as children, and ultimately reduce their compassion through overuse. When death is reduced to a numbers game, when people are ciphers being wiped from a board, of course there is no feeling. But death — your death, my death, the death of loved ones — nothing dilutes that pain.

Bill's mother died five weeks after the birth of our first child. I have since read of people, widows particularly, who somehow program themselves for their death. My mother-in-law, the widow Kate Wylie, had seen her last child married with a child of his own. Her job was done. She had two strokes, one week apart. My father, her physician, couldn't understand why she wasn't rallying. There didn't seem to be any residual damage, only a little trouble with her eyes, with focusing. On the evening of her death, we went to visit her, taking the baby (Liz) with us. Bill's mother said to my husband, "There are some things on the dresser you might need," and he took them. We were scarcely home when he was called back. The next day, after dealing with the undertaker and the final arrangements, Bill took the things out of the bag to see what his mother thought he needed: black socks and a black tie.

His mother's death separated my husband from me in a way I didn't understand. I still don't, fully, but I have observed that such self-protective isolation is almost automatic and certainly necessary. At the time I felt so shut out I thought our marriage was over. Bill closeted himself with his grief, unwilling — not unwilling, but unable — to share it. I report this now because it is another facet of grieving that must be recognized: a retreat from pain, a denial of others, a focus on one's loss. It happens most often and with the most damage to parents whose child has died. They share a loss, yet they are unable to share their grief. Again, some surveys have suggested that, following the death of a child, the incidence of marriage breakup, separation, and divorce is higher than the average. It seems we not only die alone, but also grieve alone. One learns, as always, the hard way.

My husband and I made this discovery at a vulnerable time in our marriage, with a new baby I was trying to learn how to take care of, with a new responsibility my husband was trying to learn to shoulder, along with the realization that he was an orphan.

At whatever age it comes, orphanhood devastates the psyche. I knew that, long before I became an orphan myself. Many times over the years, when I wrote friends who had lost their last parent, I commented on this change of status, in its way more crippling than the loss itself. I learned this from my husband's experience, not mine. When the last parent departs, the snipers have the survivor in their sights. Everyone else has been picked off. Standing up there in the front ranks, the eldest or among them, the leader of the party is totally vulnerable. Little by little I, you, we, all of us, become aware of our own mortality.

We had a brush with death when our youngest child was born. Matthew was only four pounds, five ounces, at birth and went into an incubator for observation. On the third day, he had a convulsion, and we were required to give permission for tests to determine the cause. If one of them proved positive, he would die. We asked for him to be baptized so he would not go nameless into that good night, and we waited for several hours for the verdict. Born without sugar in his blood, a condition easily rectified, our younger son lived, but the (brain) damage was done. Like many other parents, I have learned to live with a continuing loss, a low-grade grief.

I thought then, now Fate will spare us. We have our Trouble, we're not untouched. My father always used to warn us that when people seem to have the world by the tail, the sun always shining for them, that's when troubles come, when they're least expected. So the Wylie family had its little cross to bear — a funny way to think of our Matthew, who was no cross — but a care all the same. Who decides when one has enough on one's plate? Not me, certainly. No one is exempt from life, or from death.

Matthew was not quite four when my father died. Cancer of the liver. There are liver transplants now, but not then. Actually, the stubborn man had walked around with it for probably a year or more before he finally presented himself to another doctor for the expected diagnosis: he was given three months to live. He saw his hospital admissions, that is, his patients, in his dressing gown, a patient himself. Then he went home to hold court and say goodbye.

A terminal illness is terribly painful not only for the person who is ill and undergoing physical pain but also for the caregiver(s) who must watch the gradual and then ever-hastening disintegration, the wasting and the suffering, helpless to do anything but watch and try to help. I saw my mother almost destroy herself looking after my father, and he was quick to go. Some caregivers reach burnout after years — two, three, six, ten? — of constant daily care, with little respite. Most people want to die at home now, and most health services would rather let them because it costs so much to keep them in hospital. However, very little thought or money has been spent on the free but increasingly complex care provided by the family members, usually one, usually working alone.

That's another subject. As far as loss is concerned, and grieving, the slow, inexorability of a terminal illness is a harrowing experience for the bereaved, as hard on the physical body as it is on the spirit. The indelible pain it stamps on the soul is the chief reason why many older women who have nursed their husbands through a terminal illness to death choose not to remarry, wishing never again to go through that ordeal.

As for the devoted daughter, I found the pain of farewell to be excruciating — the knowledge that nothing I could say or do would keep my father with us. I began to understand why my husband had shut me out; my pain seemed too exquisite and too personal to share. And yet, oddly enough, when we returned to the family cottage the next summer — the place where we had been only a year earlier when we first received the news that my father would be gone before Christmas — I felt only serenity and comfort. I had said all my goodbyes; the ghosts had been laid to rest; the memories were healing ones. But I was only a daughter.

After that we lost our home town, another kind of death. Never expecting to, we left the city of our birth and of our children's, and settled in another place. That's when I stopped remembering phone numbers and began forgetting everyone's name, meeting too many strangers, having no roots. I wept in the house we had moved into, mourning the custom-designed kitchen of my dreams in the (renovated) big, old house we had left in Winnipeg. I remember asking a new, friendly neighbor to come to my funeral if I died in Stratford. I asked Bill the first time he flew away (back to Winnipeg for a wrap-up meeting) if I should stay in Stratford if he crashed. And then *he* died and my neighbor came to *his* funeral, and I stayed on in Stratford, for a while.

Easter Sunday evening, over after-dinner coffee with a guest in the living room, my husband fell forward with his head on the coffee table. The coroner said it was death by asphyxiation, but, years later, a heart specialist, hearing the story and asking for details, reckoned cardiac arrest must have blown a circuit in the system.

Bill dropped his brandy snifter, and it rolled on the carpet, and twelve-year-old brain-damaged Matthew saw it roll and talked about it for a week — of which more anon, when I discuss how death affects children.

"Life is never the same again." People say that, and then it happens, it strikes home, that is, it strikes one's life companion and it's all true. Life is never the same again. As a matter of fact, it never was, it never will be, it always changes, but somehow, before this major fact sinks in and is absorbed as truth, one could think or pretend, as I did, that life was safer than that, that it was the same, always and forever, the same, only different. Changing, yes, but the same. It's not.

Here is the cutting edge. Here is the fine line between public attitudes and private assimilation. Not fine — huge, a crevasse, in fact, the abyss that yawns between one's private pain and the world and its assumptions. This is the knowledge that must be grasped and internalized, that loss is change and change is constant. *Nothing is ever the same.*

This account was supposed to be about death, but it's about other losses, necessarily. Matthew hit a Catch-22 in his life just before his seventeenth birthday and went into a downward spiral of anxiety and depression. He spent three months in the Clarke Institute in Toronto and another nine months at home recovering, before he made a slow comeback. Facing his own loss of sanity and all the losses that accompany it, both public and private, he said, on the verge of recovery, "I have to jump back into the future."

I have to jump back into the future.

We all have to, although at the time I wanted to jump back into the past. At no time does a single parent miss the other, departed parent as much as when their child faces deep trouble. The soul then knows how alone one is.

My mother died five years after I moved to Toronto, just five months after she moved from Winnipeg to live down the hall where I could take care of her. The mothers and daughters of my generation had their troubles with each other, and we were not exempt. I will deal with this later in more depth. For now I will simply say that I had become a full orphan, up there at the top of the family tree now, a matriarch, the next to go, in all likelihood. The air up there isn't thin; it's thick with responsibility. If one has lived long enough, there's not much fear.

What of one's own death? Most of us think we're immortal until proved wrong. For some, this proof is a long time coming. Close but not fatal encounters with death have their effect. The change is one of direction, as of a weather vane that turns with the wind. Those who have been brushed by death and return no longer hang on so tightly to life. They seem to have a different orientation, different goals than those who still foster their illusions of immortality. Not that these people are morbid or show despair; on the contrary, they are frequently more enthusiastic, more patient, more authentic, tougher but more gentle than they ever used to be. Something internal has happened to them and they have changed. This change has to do with the discovery of the loss of self.

The other change takes place in people who have lost their most significant other. (Such a strange term, this modern coining for reference to one's life companion, but it serves well.) The change occurs in two steps, both of them Giant, and painful. First of all, one discovers that one is not immortal, not through the evidence of one's own body but through the loss of one that has been, as the phrase goes, "flesh of my flesh, blood of my blood, bone of my bone." One learns that no one is spared death, not even when protected by love. So much for immortality. The loss is of illusion.

The other change is more deeply internal, less intellectual, more deeply felt, and to describe it I must tell my own story again. As sometimes happens to survivors, I had a death wish following the death of my husband. I didn't express it overtly, at least not aloud to my friends or children, but it was there, a constant companion to my thoughts, and I was aware of it. I found when I was driving on the highway I would have a sudden urge to swerve into the path of an oncoming car. How simple it would be: one big bang and it would be over. What prevented me was concern for the other driver and passengers, not any fear for myself. It would be unfair to take someone else with me, far too selfish. But I still kept thinking it.

Less than a year after Bill had died, I was driving back to Toronto from Stratford, bringing my older daughter, by then at university, and her roommate home for the weekend. A freezing rain had turned Highway 401 into a skating rink. Passing a truck, I felt a sudden down-draft of air push the car sideways; I went into a long skid, out of control. The truck slowed to allow me to take over the road. I spun across the highway into the median strip, which fortunately, at that point, was deep enough that I didn't keep going across it and into the lanes of oncoming traffic. The nose of the car settled into a declivity that prevented further progress. I turned off the motor, and sighed.

Leaving the two young women in the car, I hitchhiked to the nearest service station; came back in a tow truck, which pulled the car out of the ditch, and then drove on to Stratford. We were late, but there was no damage done to any of us, including the car. Another hour found me in bed, picking up my diary for my nightly report, a compulsive habit since my husband's death. I read the last lines from the night before, not remembering what I had written. "Dear God," I read, "when can I die too?"

Any time, the answer seemed to be. Any time you want. It's as easy as that. That's when I decided I had to be more careful with my children's only parent.

But I knew the wish was still there every time I flew. As the plane took off I would acknowledge that, yes, I was ready to go and it would be just fine, I didn't mind at all. Then I would do a quick mental check of my will and other arrangements and come up short with the reminder that Matt still needed me. I couldn't leave yet. Once, on a trip to Scotland to meet his father's side of the family, Matt was with me. We encountered some severe turbulence, and I automatically swung into my mental checklist. When I got to Matthew, I remembered that he was with me this time, so I turned to him and said, "It's okay if we crash, Matt. We're together." He looked at me in total dismay. "Come on!" he said. He didn't want to die. That brought me back sharply.

I can remember the exact moment and circumstances of leaving my death wish, or of my death wish leaving me. I had been invited to the Writers' Workshop at the Arts Centre in Banff, Alberta: six uninterrupted weeks of writing, with peers and mentors to discuss it. Introductions and orientation over, the third night (about 9:00 p.m.), I was sitting on my bed, reading and thinking, making notes on the work I was doing, when suddenly a deep joy flooded me, accompanied by a conviction that I was doing what I wanted, what I was intended to do. I was not merely marking time until I could go too. I had work to do. Suddenly I wanted to go on living.

Like rings in a tree or notches in a gunbelt are all these changes, proof that I have lived and loved a long time, enough to have suffered most of life's losses, and survived. I am offering my *curriculum vitae* partly to illustrate my qualifications for writing this book, but also to conjure memories of similar experiences in my readers. We cannot touch a universal verity if we have not felt the specific truth in our own lives. What we are to make of it all remains to be seen.

3. A Survey of Death

Any man's death diminishes me, because I am involved in mankind;
and therefore never send to know for whom the bell tolls;
it tolls for thee.
—JOHN DONNE

IN THE MIDDLE AGES NO ONE HAD TO SEND OUT TO HEAR for whom the bell tolled; next time, for sure, it would be for thee, or me. If not now, then later, but, in any case, soon. Death may have been expected, but it wasn't welcome; it was always accursed. It was the constant fly in the ointment, the reminder that no matter who one was or what one possessed, death lay in wait. The grinning skull always lay behind the mask of flesh, no matter how beautiful or pampered that flesh. Dust and ashes and mortality silted up the houses of the rich as well as of the poor, piling up in the corners and lurking behind the door.

Memento mori was the reminder: remember, you're going to die. Who could forget? Anyone who stopped to listen could hear Time's winged chariot hurrying near; the meter was running all the time. (Not that we don't hear the ticking even now, but we have given ourselves a greater opportunity to ignore it.) In his book *The Making of the Modern Family*, Edward Shorter reports on the method of circulating the news of a death in Catholic villages in centuries past; the example is Catholic because there was a church with a bell already in use for the daily Angelus. "There would be sixteen rings for a man, twelve for a woman. . . . In theory, as the bells tolled, the village's inhabitants would pause to say a prayer." The prayers were frequent.

Life expectancy in the Middle Ages was something under forty years, less for women, who died in childbirth with such appalling regularity that the tales of the brothers Grimm were filled with gruesome episodes involving nasty stepmothers. Part of the reason for such low figures for life expectancy was that so few babies lived to adulthood: two out of four died in the first year of life and usually one of the remaining two before maturity.

For adults, the hour of death was an awesome, observed occasion, the final reckoning and preparation for eternity. People gathered to say goodbye ("God be wi' ye — and with thy spirit") and to receive forgiveness, if necessary (it usually was), from the living and from God. Last wishes were uttered, and some famous last words. Everyone paid attention. (I'm talking about the upper and the beginning of the middle classes; for the peasantry, life was as cheap and unmarked then as now.)

This death was what Philippe Ariès in his book, *The Hour of Our Death*, describes as the "tame death." When life was short and death was expected, it was accompanied by familiar rites and ceremonies, and publicly attended. Death took place at home, within familiar walls, and burial too, within walls, with protection provided by the prayers of the family and the blessing of the church. By Victorian times, the age of "the beautiful death" arrived. The grinning skull adopted a decorous smile as it hovered in the bedrooms of the dying. Death still occurred at home but it was labeled good rather than accursed.

Tame or good, death was always a social and public fact. The entire community was affected by it and paused to pay their respects. Sometimes it was a public performance, as in the execution of a criminal. Crowds would go to witness the hanging of a highwayman or the beheading of a political prisoner. In rural communities even until recently, death was out in the open — under the wheels of a tractor — or familiar and close — in the front bedroom.

Gradually "the institutional death" took over. The deathbed scene was transferred to the hospital, discreetly at first, in the 1930s and 1940s, then more commonly after 1950. Disease, not death, was the diagnosis, with a promise of recovery. People frequently did recover, but when the doctors and drugs and hospitals failed, death became an isolated secret, solitary and shameful. People were cheated of their awe and of their final peacemaking. A hospital, after all, is in the business of health. Its efficient medicine, its aseptic perfection, its relentlessly cheerful optimism, its sterile hygiene — none of these allows for the messy promiscuity of death.

In his landmark article (1955) about the "pornography of death," Geoffrey Gorer showed that death had become as concealed as sex was in Victorian times. In 1963, Gorer conducted a survey that revealed that only a quarter of the bereaved had been present at the death of a close relative. Death not only was shameful, but had become a very private act.

Dame Cicely Saunders and Elisabeth Kübler-Ross began to change this with palliative care. Saunders began her hospice services for the terminally ill in Britain, Kübler-Ross in the United States. Focusing on the family as the primary unit of care, working in tandem with the professionals (Kübler-Ross is a doctor), they reestablished the idea of the good death. In addition to the comfort and reassurance the service provided, this concept reminds the dying and their families of the spiritual side of human beings' search for meaning in life.

Ironically, what began as a superintensive, private-care concept has been adopted and extended by hospitals as an economical means of letting people die, with more inexpensive, amateur (family and volunteer) help and less expensive professional (doctors, nurses, hospital equipment) care. What began as a rejection of isolated institutional death has become an embracing of home deaths — so much more human and so much less of a drain on government funds. Perhaps death has become private and human again, that is, if it's the right kind of death, after a long terminal illness that allows for extended farewells. Death with dignity — that's the catch phrase these days. Dying with dignity, according to the central character in the 1979 movie *All That Jazz*, means you don't drool.

At the same time, we're making the most serious bid for immortality, or something approaching it, that we have ever made. Geneticists and biologists are talking about extending the life span to one hundred or more healthy years. The motto of some doctors these days would seem to be immortality at any cost, or at least prolonged life, no matter what the quality of the life sustained. Unnatural, elaborate, and often painful means of life support are used to keep a patient in an uncomfortable twilight zone between life and death. Similarly, damaged infants are being overtreated by physicians who take their Hippocratic Oath seriously: to maintain, to save lives at all costs. Ethics committees are springing up in hospitals all over the country as doctors and lawyers and humanists struggle to determine what constitutes unnatural treatment, to mediate the patients' and families' right either to refuse treatment or to grant consent, and ultimately to attempt to define death.

Euthanasia, so-called mercy killing, is a very dirty word. When is pulling a plug euthanasia and when is it simply eliminating a therapy? Perhaps when the person doesn't die, as in the case of Karen Quinlan who lived for nine years in a coma after her respirator was removed. Apart from the consultations between medic and next-of-kin, what about the private agreement between the dying one and the survivor? I have read moving stories of deaths requested by the patient and aided by lover, adult child, or mate. In cases like these, great care must be taken to distinguish between depression caused by an illness that may not be fatal (yet) and the truly final, pain-filled days. It's not easy to play God. No one is omniscient.

In one such case, a husband, identified only as "Derek" in the book *Widower*, describes the assistance he gave his wife, at her request, to enable her to die before her cancer of the marrow finished her. He reports his subsequent wild expressions of grief, and his decision to publish a book about his experiences. He ended up becoming a spokesman for euthanasia and in 1980 founded the Hemlock Society, "to argue for the right to die and the right to assistance in death" — now a national organization with over 13,000 members. No comment, except maybe a line from the Roman writer Cato: "It were as ignoble to beg death . . . as to beg life."

4. Styles in Mourning

To church; and with my mourning, very handsome, and new periwig,
make a great show.
—SAMUEL PEPYS, *DIARY*, MARCH 21, 1667

IN TIMES PAST, WHEN RITUAL PRESCRIBED THE DEATHBED,
it also laid down the rules for proper, decent conduct following the
death. Mourning rituals were observed and respected not only by the
immediate family but also by the entire community. Certainly then as
now there were bereaved persons who felt not a particle of pain at the
passing of a mate; deep mourning smacked of hypocrisy to them and to
those who knew their true feelings. But now the simulation required
reverses old behavior patterns: those who really care and who suffer bitter
pain must endure their agony in secret so as not to embarrass others.
Hardest hit of all are those whose emotions about the departed were
ambivalent or who had unfinished business, unresolved love–hate problems that are difficult to work through when half the equation is missing.

Mourning always used to begin with the deathbed scene. Anyone
who has seen a Hollywood movie knows something of the old approach
to death. Families group, sobbing, around the dying one. Everyone prays
for the departing soul, or at least kneels and looks solemn. The priest
leads a somber little procession—at least two altar boys, a swinging
incense burner, with a small choir in the background singing plainsong—
come to administer the last rites and prepare the sinner's soul to meet
the Almighty. (This is Hollywood High Church.)

And then there was the funeral: great swags of black velvet, held in place by gleaming white skulls, and huge arrangements of white lilies adorn the church, which resonates with the voices of a massed choir (this is a high funeral mass — very high). Lighted candles everywhere, and more incense (used originally to protect the nose from the smell of the decaying body), the organ music swelling and lifting awed spirits to a glorious reconciliation with death. The trip to the cemetery was a parade: proud black stallions plumed in black or violet, pulling a gleaming black hearse, followed by a cortege en route to the burying place. Great marble dwellings waited for the dead of titled families, with bowed stone mourners and trumpeting angels marking their way. The bodies were laid to their final rest on marble slabs rather than in wooden boxes in the earth, or, if in coffins, in stone ones with carved effigies on the lids above their decaying mortal remains. The stone houses echoed with more tears and howls and sobbing prayers rising and hovering like incense over week-long vigils. Great flaming torches lit the way to dusty death as the bereaved expressed their final farewells in eloquent and cautionary words.

Ashes to ashes and dust to dust, intoned the priest or rabbi or minister. In orthodox Judaism the naked body would be wrapped in a sheet and laid in a simple, unadorned box within twenty-four hours of the death, while the mourners' clothes were slashed and the mirrors sheeted to prevent the spirit's entrapment.

Hollywood and I have got it all mixed up, condensing several centuries' and a couple of continents' treatment of death. We share in the Judeo-Christian perspective, with a Victorian hangover. But this confusion is still somehow what we expect to happen. In reality, the modern approach — not an approach, an evasion, a refusal to confront the facts of death — is quite different. Funeral and burial styles have changed.

Embalming, for those who allow it, eliminates the need for incense; a little motor and smooth pulleys lower the coffin more painlessly than the pallbearers' muscles; flat markers provide little information other than the names and dates, while perpetual care turns the cemetery into a faceless park, at least in the new sections. A funeral director recently told me that in his city in the last ten years, cremation, which used to account for 15 percent of all his funerals, now represents 52 percent.

The changes are not all bad, but they are very different from the earlier style. I recently heard of a memorial gesture that involved the scattering of a man's ashes at sea from the stern of his beloved schooner. That had some sense of ceremony to it.

I was told of another man, a proclaimed agnostic who wanted no part of ceremony or ritual, whose similarly unbelieving friends honored his wishes and engaged no minister. Instead, they whistled a tune over him, broke the tin whistle, and threw it on the casket before they took turns with the spade. When they were finished, they each took a swig of good Scotch and poured the rest of the bottle as a libation over the grave. If that isn't ceremony, I don't know what is.

We seem to agree with the past on one thing: mourning begins with the funeral. There are only a few rituals left. We have the "visitation," the get-together at the undertaker's a night or so before the funeral when the survivor has to act like the mother (or father) of the bride, the perfect host, setting people at their ease. Jews still sit shiva following the immediate burial of the body. Shiva is like a long (seven-day), quiet wake of talking and paying respects. The more orthodox "sit low," that is, on low stools or chairs, as a symbol of how low they have been brought by death. Jews don't practice cremation; even if they don't always sheet their mirrors, they don't use them to shave or apply makeup for a week after the death, and while clothes may not be slashed, a token cloth or ribbon is still cut as a symbol of the rending of garments.

The funeral is the one common ritual of mourning that remains to us. People know what to do about funerals: they go to them. If they have some acquaintance with the bereaved family, they also go to some sort of a post-funeral reception at the family home. They express their grief and pay their respects and leave. That's it. Duty done, respects paid, most of them bury memory as well. They leave the bereaved high, but not dry, with an empty space the size of a gravel pit. The funeral is all we have left that defines an all-too-brief mourning period and sets a limit on it. Too small a definition, too tight a limitation. In the quiet of the house the day after the funeral, with the heavy fragrance of dying flowers lying in the silent air, the survivor(s) must begin the mourning that others think is passed, finished, completed.

Where ceremony leaves off and confusion begins for everyone is the denial of any genuine mourning period to the bereaved. One week after the final burial or scattering or libation or rending, as the case may be, the ones who are left behind are expected to get on with their lives. If they must indulge themselves in some physical expression of grief, best to indulge in private so as not to embarrass others.

No one wears black any more. Mourning clothes and colors and symbols used to be strictly prescribed: black clothes for the families of the bereaved, both male and female, then black armbands for the men and black dresses for the women for at least the first year, succeeded by somber gray, and no bright colors for the remainder of a widow's life; black or violet (in memory of Grandmama) for children; black wreaths on the doors. Some families even clung to the old tradition of sheeting their mirrors. Following a death in the immediate family, custom dictated more than the outward vestments. Social behavior was strictly coded and enforced: no feasts, no parties, no dancing. Look at the trouble Scarlett O'Hara got into when she broke the rules!

There is no longer any prescribed code of behavior, except, perhaps, that of reticence. One is supposed never to show emotion or pain, or be so indiscreet as to cry. Tears, after all, might be contagious, and no one wants to catch them. "Society," says Philippe Ariès, "refuses to participate in the emotion of the bereaved. . . . [It] regards mourning as morbid."

According to most funeral directors and everything I have observed and discovered, a funeral still performs three major functions. First, it helps the bereaved ("the funeral is for us"). It convinces them, as nothing else, that the loved one has, in fact, died. People differ in their feelings about open caskets (they're not permitted in the Jewish religion). My husband wanted a closed one, one of the few things we had ever discussed in connection with death, but I kept it open for my immediate family's private service, to help convince the children and me that their father was dead. People who hold a memorial service in the absence of a body have trouble with reality. Without a body, the survivor retains some illusion that the departed is still on this earth, somewhere, and might return.

The funeral, as nothing else, thrusts the bereaved into the new role that must be played—in fact, not so much a role, I would venture, as a cage, with a label identifying markings, habitat, range: *Black-breasted widow, found in grocery stores, churches, lunchrooms and parlors, in the company of other widows and sometimes children*, or, *Dark-browed widower, found in offices and bars, in the company of other golfers and sometimes younger women.*

The second major function of a funeral is to give people a chance to acknowledge publicly the loss in their midst and to express their emotions in an acceptable way — not always easy, especially, I want to say, for men. One of my husband's closest friends could not say anything to my face. Instead, he phoned me, though he was in the same city, and poured out his almost incoherent anguish and rage, sobbing over the telephone as he could never have done in my presence. Public ritual helps people to a formal, nonthreatening expression of this kind of emotional outpouring.

It is for this reason that we see an honor guard of police officers marching at a murdered fellow officer's funeral; that the president and his wife attend the memorial service for fallen astronauts; that, even now, when lying-in-state is no longer customary, thousands file by or sing along or engage in some form of mass mourning for an influential, powerful figure in politics, sports, or entertainment. Society's group values are upheld by such public demonstrations. Not only is death kept at bay and continuing life asserted, but evildoers are warned (in the case of the murdered policeman, for example): no one is going to tolerate this kind of death. We are not resigned.

Everyone will acknowledge that the third major function of the ritual surrounding funerals is an economic one: the exchange of services we usually dismiss as simply being a good neighbor. This aspect of community mourning remains very much intact. People still send flowers and food to the bereaved family and provide practical assistance: accommodation for the out-of-town mourners, child care, kitchen help, telephone answering and message-taking, chauffeuring — myriad acts of practical help, the expression of sympathy and concern in action.

This wealth of goods and services is expected to be reciprocated. The next time death knocks, it may be at the neighbor's door, and then those who have received help will rally round and proffer the same assistance. It's the least they can do, they say, and they're right. Such mutual help is a way of expressing gratitude, not only to the living but to the dead.

Hans Selye developed an entire philosophy of life based on such gratitude. His theory of altruism explains why people perform acts of kindness and generosity, not only on a small, human, daily basis but in a large-scale way, such as bequests, legacies, endowments, monuments, and so on. The Bible tells us that the sins of the fathers are visited on the sons (no mention of the debts incurred by mothers and daughters); Selye's theory reassuringly suggests that the *gifts* of the deceased will be extended to their posterity, and that gratitude continues into subsequent generations. The behavior of people at funerals admirably supports this theory. When I think of the casseroles and baking and assistance of all kinds that poured in upon me at the time of my husband's death, I am still weak with gratitude, and I have been trying ever since to express that gratitude to others. "Pass it on" is an expression we all know. Like a stone thrown in a pond, an act of kindness can send ripples out to an entire community — the world? — in time.

Most of the wishes of the deceased are honored in the funeral rites, that is, the choice of burial (or scattering) place, hymns to be sung, poetry to be read — in short, the celebration. Most memorable was the colorful celebration Jim Henson (creator of *Sesame Street* and the Muppets) produced from beyond the grave.

In any case, whether cloaked in black or televised in color, this kind of ritual attending mourning, one of the few remaining, is immensely comforting to the survivors. Best of all, it shows that when people know what to do, they do it.

I deal in parables: a little boy was stricken when his dog was killed, run over by a car. The day after the accident, the boy's parents suggested they go to a pet store and get him a new puppy. "Not yet," said the boy, "I have to miss Rags first." He knew he needed to mourn.

There is another lesson in this story, too: simple swift replacement of the lost love object doesn't work. A lot of adults (mostly men) try to do this after the death of a spouse. It's the point of the story in Neil Simon's play *Chapter Two*, about a widower who remarries too soon and who, Simon thinks, can't accept happiness. What is really wrong is that he hasn't gone through a mourning period.

So how does one express sorrow? The important word is express:

Give sorrow words; the grief that does not speak
Whispers the o'er-fraught heart and bids it break.
—WILLIAM SHAKESPEARE, *MACBETH* IV, iii, 209–10

This, of course, is what twentieth-century psychologists have been saying all along, that people must give vent to their feelings, and that they must be allowed, even encouraged, to do so. We still haven't considered how. It's easier for the articulate. They have to touch their feelings with words in order to recognize their own emotions. They just naturally have to talk about how they feel and, in so doing, ease the mourning. But what about those to whom words do not come easily, who find real difficulty in asking for the butter, let alone commenting on how the pain inside is burning them alive? They need breathing space. Good mourning provides that breathing space.

Music sometimes helps to express mourning, sometimes not. One thinks of all the inspiring requiems composed in the past to mourn someone's death — Christ's, mostly, but those of kings and queens and princes of the realm. Mozart's last great work was a requiem mass (not quite completed when he died). All composers, I am told, even in this sterile century, want to create at least one requiem in their lifetime. American composer Leonard Bernstein wrote a requiem that strikes me as more dramatic than moving; Canadian composer Peter Bering has written a more traditional one, though the music is modern. But these are the creators. One is not expected to create when in the throes of mourning, is one?

I have known many people who survived the first months of a mourning period solely through music. They developed a ritual of their own. They spoke to no one unnecessarily and they wrapped themselves in sound, in a cocoon of music. Music applied topically to an emotional wound can, indeed, contribute to healing. Among the people I have observed, melancholy and sentimental pop music seems to work best for the end of a relationship, even divorce. The awesome finality of death requires more: spirituals, hymns, and psalms performed by magnificent choirs, or the exalted passions and requiems written by the giants: Bach, Beethoven, Mozart. Not to make too sweeping a generalization, I hasten to add that the choice of music depends on the personality of the sufferer. I do state generically that music should be part of the prescribed treatment for mourning.

We need so much after this personal firestorm has struck our lives. When the smoke clears, if there's one person singed but upright — or, perhaps, a little bent, doubled over, in fact, with pain — then that person has to begin again. You, I, we — have to start over. First we have to mourn, then we have to grieve.

I am fully aware that the thesaurus pegs *to mourn* and *to grieve* as synonymous, but I intend to separate them in time and in purpose. First comes mourning, then comes grieving. Mourning is a backward mechanism, filling in the hole, shovelling the earth on the coffin, as it were, while grieving is a forward process, gathering strength and new skills. Grieving (I'll say it again) is a creative process.

> mourn *vb. (from an Indo-European root meaning to remember), to feel sorrow, grief, or regret, to lament, deplore, bewail; to show the conventional signs of grief for a period following a person's death.*
> — *OXFORD ENGLISH DICTIONARY*, THIRD EDITION

Let us set aside *grieve* for now and get on with mourning. One of the reasons for encoded mourning periods in the past was that people needed time for the initial healing of the wound to begin. The reason is still valid. We are surely all agreed that the loss is like a wound, sometimes a massive amputation, sometimes a mere scratch, a slight blow, but a wound nonetheless. The blood clots, the first scar tissue forms, surface tenderness eases, the deep bruises begin to unlock. A ritually prescribed mourning grants the time for such basic healing to take place. Without it, without the immobilization and some favoring treatment, the wound won't heal properly, or as quickly, and there will never be any comfort.

> *"Blessed are they that mourn: for they shall be comforted."*
> — MATTHEW 5:4

Lament. Some people, some nationalities, seem to be more practised and less self-conscious than others about sobbing out their pain and screaming at their misery. It's time cold, stiff-upper-lip WASPs acquired this proficiency. They might develop fewer ulcers and festering wounds if they did. The image of Jackie Kennedy rises before us all, controlled, ladylike, well-bred, beautifully behaved in the face of an overwhelming loss laced with horror and violence. Admirable though she was, she did us all a disservice. She became the model of behavior for a generation of widows: cool, calm, collected, masking her own pain, putting others at their ease, bearing up. Surely, in this third stage of feminism in the twentieth century, we must be allowed, and allow ourselves, to cry, to mourn.

Lament, lamentation — the word itself bespeaks another century. Again, for me, music: "Asa's Lament" from Grieg's *Peer Gynt*. The wild, repetitious rush of the opening strains of that lament remind me of the first despairing throes of grief when the mind attacks the terrifying walls of pain closing in on it and claws at their frustrating blankness. The root word of *lament* means "bark." Yes, bark at the moon.

To mourn is also to deplore, to disapprove of. Edna St. Vincent Millay, in her poem "Dirge Without Music," which begins "I am not resigned to the shutting away of loving hearts in the hard ground," expresses precisely the restrained, anguished deploring that characterizes keen mourning:

> *Gently they go, the beautiful, the tender, the kind;*
> *Quietly they go, the intelligent, the witty, the brave.*
> *I know. But I do not approve. And I am not resigned.*

"Not resigned." Loss takes a long time to get used to, if that ever happens. Not resigned. But it might be wise to give mourning a chance, to give mourners a chance to mourn, to become resigned.

Mourners in the past were identifiable by the clothes they wore and, in the early stages, by their seclusion. They were not expected to reenter the social whirl too soon; in fact, it was frowned upon if they did. It's safer that way. I can remember running to a bedroom to cry because a stranger at a party, having no way of knowing my situation, dropped a casual remark that hurt me. Soon after that I removed my wedding and engagement rings so as to avoid being asked where my husband was and seeing others recoil at my reply. I realized soon, however, how much I was to blame for the encounters that rankled my feelings and left me bitter and angry at unsuspecting, innocent people who made the mistake of going on with their own lives. I had this chip labeled "Self-Pity" on one shoulder and this two-by-four labeled "Resentment" on the other, and no one could do right by me. I was uppermost in my mind and I expected to be uppermost in others' as well. It never works that way.

Not to say that a society that allowed a little more mourning time or at least one that recognized the need for it, wouldn't be helpful. The bereaved must be allowed to lick their wounds.

Thus I make the distinction between mourning and grieving. Mourning is gesture, necessary gesture; grieving is process. Basically, the act of mourning represents the emotional disruption of normality. If it can be coded and defined, it can offer a clearer way through the first fogs and mists of pain and fear accompanying any major change in life, particularly the death of a loved one. If mourning is not permitted, if the rules of behavior have been lost, then in all likelihood the mourner will be lost as well.

Grieving is a long-term project, a working-out, a coming-to-terms. Certainly emotion is involved, painful emotion. Grieving is a tougher, longer process, and very hard work. But it cannot be successfully addressed until due attention has been paid to mourning. The successful, healthy, unrushed completion of mourning paves the way for the grieving process, although the two may (for a time) go on simultaneously. Toby Talbot, in *A Book About My Mother*, describes a time when she tried to console her four-year-old daughter who was weeping bitterly about something that had upset her:

"In trying to comfort her, I brushed the tears from her cheeks. Her sobs immediately converted into an angered outcry: 'Give me back my tears!' "

Give me back my tears.

5. Attitudes to Death

People who are afraid of living are also especially frightened of death.
— MEDARD BOSS

SOCIETY'S ATTITUDES TO DEATH HAVE CHANGED OVER THE centuries. People's perception of death was directly related to their faith, or lack of it. At one time, though death was cruel and swift and early, everyone was assured of eternal life — in Heaven, if one was good. Part of the terror of death was the possibility of Hell waiting on the other side.

Even in Victorian times, death was final, but not too final. The expectation hovered that all of us would meet in the sweet by-and-by. Even America's most brilliant psychologist-scientist, William James, dabbled in spiritualism and tried through a medium to get in touch with the disembodied spirits of his parents. Everyone was supposed to die in the arms of the Creator; washed in the blood of the Lamb, sinners and saints alike were to enjoy life in the Promised Land. Death was desirable, especially for those poor souls who had no happiness or wealth on this side of the Pearly Gates. The promise of better things to come kept most of them docile here on earth. Hellfire and brimstone, the grimacing skull, and the triumphant anticipatory satanic leer did not pose the terrible, tangible threats they had done in earlier centuries; the devil retreated to Hallowe'en with the other spooks while all the liberated souls danced with the Lord of the Dance.

Not that there wasn't pain associated with death. It has always hurt to be parted from one's loved ones, perhaps more so when there was so little that could be done to save them, when life was so precarious and so brief. However, in these days of miracle drugs, we tend to feel cheated when someone dies, we think, too soon. We do not bow so easily or with such serenity to fate as we might once have done.

The death of a child was not nearly the tragedy it is in our antiseptic, birth-controlled society where (theoretically) every child is a desired one. In his book *The Making of the Modern Family*, Edward Shorter forcefully illustrates the parental indifference to infants in the eighteenth and nineteenth centuries. With a fifty-fifty chance at life for infants, Shorter insists, parents tended to withdraw emotionally and psychologically from the pain involved. Few people can sustain loss after loss with impunity. Considering the harshness of life, Shorter even suggests that "death would be perceived as a blessing for both children and parents." Anonymous and plentiful, children were often not named until they were three or four or twelve months old. Why waste a perfectly good name on, or get attached to, someone who might not live? If a child was named, he might receive a number as well: Joseph I, Joseph II, Joseph III, and so on, until, perhaps, Joseph IV or V lived. If names were thus interchangeable, so were their bearers. Angels guided the little nameless bairns to their rest.

It has to do with focus. We still feel the same way about children: we care a lot if we happen to know their names. Thus, one child who falls down a well captures the attention and sympathy of millions who watch her rescue on the national news while the United Nation's statement that five days' worth of defense spending (about two billion dollars) would feed the planet's hungry children for five years is met with a collective shrug. A Wish Foundation, which grants dying kids their last fantasies is enthusiastically subscribed to while the effort to provide all children with clean water or across-the-board immunization remains a weary struggle.

Those are examples of the compartmentalization of our thinking, having to do with focus, but perhaps more with control, or the lack of it. One death we can handle, do something about, feel as if it's manageable; more than that — entire populations wiped out by famine or flood — leaves us feeling helpless. So with this century's approach to death; it's not solely a denial of death but an attempt to gain control of it. There's a course in miracles to help people with AIDS find inner peace and healing; there's Simonton imaging: battling cancer cells metaphorically, thus arming the body psychically against the disease. There's the whole range of holistic medicine designed to help us limp sturdily into the sunset with our doctor and our spiritual mentor as joint guides. It's all so *hygienic* and preposterous. People who commit the social gaffe of being really sick, and who fail to respond to their doctors' efforts to cure them, are hidden away to die in antiseptic rooms, out of sight of their families and society. Death, once a public fact, respected and observed by the entire community, has become a taboo. If one has to die, at least have the decency to do it gracefully, and if not gracefully, then discreetly, and if not discreetly, then quickly, and if not quickly, then eloquently, with deathbed scenes rivalling those of Dickens in their completeness and beauty. Those suffering extreme pain are offered pain-killing "cocktails" and are praised for their nobility as they slip away down the dark passage.

Come away, come away, megatrendy death! We seem to be willing to try anything in order to go gently, gracefully, almost unconsciously into that good night, without feeling a thing.

I have a hunch that we would do better to honor death than to trivialize it. The radical French physician Ivan Illich comments that "once a culture is deprived of its death, it loses its health." We do seem to be suffering from a terrible schism between sorrow and self-control. Two approaches to death present themselves: to exit with a stiff upper lip or to fade out with a quivering lower one. Are those the only choices we have? Surely not. It's this dearth of choice that leads straight into the denial of mourning. If the departure wasn't genuine, how can mourning be authentic?

Nowadays, with angels and devils the stuff of movies, and the promise of Heaven or the threat of Hell scarcely taken seriously, death strikes most people as a fearful ignominy, an assault, an affront, a mortal insult. Today, less than half the population consoles itself with a vision of an afterlife. We have such finite perceptions we cannot conceive of infinite life outside our space–time. Most of us can't be comforted with the thought of pink clouds and angels and harps. As for Hell, it doesn't seem to exist any more. About all that most of us can manage to agree on about eternity and a significant afterlife is that there is some preservation and continuation of energy. Mass changes, scientists tell us; energy remains, it just takes different forms. Theologians who stub their souls on the question of the afterlife come up with theories ranging from corporeal survival (the kind the ancient Egyptians and Vikings, among others, expected, judging by their well-equipped pyramids and ships) to a kind of communal consciousness with all the ethereal spirits warming their impalpable hands at the central flame.

Life-after-life stories abound now. People who have "died" and returned tell of white light and benign presences greeting them, sort of a heavenly Welcome Wagon. Strangely, at the time of my husband's death, though I had read none of the stories others tell, I must admit I experienced this light and beneficence vicariously for about thirty-six hours after Bill left, a clear vision that he was taking me with him as far as was allowed into a white world filled with ineffable light. When he went on, I returned to my darkness and the necessity of slugging out my mortal time.

The Nobel prize–winning author Pearl Buck speculated about the afterlife when her husband died. She decided she didn't want to decide: "I really do not want to know the truth. If he exists it will make the waiting alone intolerable. And I cannot bear to know that he does not exist. Let me wait until I find out for myself, through experience."

People who have worked with the dying have observed in them a transcendent peace, as if indeed they were going on a desirable journey to another space. Elisabeth Kübler-Ross has translated this serenity into a conviction that something lies beyond: "Death is the final stage of growth in this life. There is no total death. Only the body dies. The self or spirit . . . is eternal. You may interpret this in any way that makes you comfortable."

Comfort, that's the key word. All this is like chicken soup; it doesn't hurt, it might help, but it doesn't go very far to make up for the fact of death. Small wonder, then, that mourning is swept under the carpet. It seems wisest to concentrate on the life at hand and ignore what lies beyond. Few people have much sympathy, anyway, for mystics and visionaries, even less for the visibly suffering. The bereaved, after all, are constant reminders of someone's mortality, reminders most people would rather do without or at least ignore. This attitude has characterized recent public attitudes to death.

Somewhere along the way a lie began to take shape, one that still influences our thinking. Imminent death, threatening death, sweet death wasn't supposed to happen.

- "He passed away in his sleep."
- "She never felt a thing."
- "He never saw it coming."
- "She looks lovely, doesn't she? — So natural."

These are the words still murmured in funeral homes, one of the reasons that some people hate open caskets. Perhaps, if the casket is open, one hears oneself agreeing, "Yes, the deceased does look so natural," as if one were discussing a still life. As Philippe Ariès has said, "This is the first time in history that a whole society has honored the dead by pretending that they were alive." Let's hear it for the morticians! As for the visitors, they behave impeccably, like hospital staff: unemotional, detached, sympathetic, self-controlled, but welcoming any comfort the bereaved can offer. All very confusing.

Death is no longer awesome; it is indecent and dirty, shameful, even déclassé. Dying is an anti-social act. Anyone who has the temerity to die is guilty of some terrible oversight. Fatal disease is not only unseemly and anti-social, it is fearful, disgusting, nauseating, and — worst of all — unattractive. Sick people are ugly, best hidden away in shame and silence in a hospital while the family goes on with normal life. (Palliative care has changed some of this.)

And if I choose to die well, wrapping my tattered rags of pride about me, who's to say I won't drool? The ambivalence is killing me. Right now, at this particular time, we all seem to be a bundle of contradictions. Anyway, I'm not the one who's dying. All those other people, they're the ones who are dying, not me. I'm just standing/sitting/lying here, watching the world pass by. When it's my turn, when I really go, I'll scarcely notice. Or will I? That's the catch, the Catch-22, in this whole messy business of death. When we feel this way, how can we be of any comfort or use to the bereaved?

Dying with dignity has become an art form, and good mental hygiene before and after bereavement is the emotional equivalent of the aerobic workout. The emotions may be well exercised; the soul needs food. The trouble is that most of what we are offered is fodder without real nourishment.

It's all mixed up in our minds. Most of us go for the stiff upper lip in public but we're not above a little hand-wringing or a few hugs from very close friends and as many tears as we can allow ourselves in private. We do agree with Freud's idea that we have to withdraw our investment in the dead one in order to regain our emotional autonomy. We know that repressed mourning can be very damaging, can, in fact, result in illness, both physical and mental, down the line. If we follow a checklist, tick off the stages of grief, work through the step-by-step process, surely we will come out on the other side restored, heart whole, and ready to keep on keeping on. We want to do things right.

II

THE GRIEVING PROCESS

Step by step, day by day, drop by drop,
grief must be worked through.

6. The Symptoms of Grief

How frighteningly few are the persons whose death would spoil our
appetite and make the world seem empty.
— ERIC HOFFER

THIS WON'T TAKE LONG. I WANT TO IDENTIFY THE SYMPTOMS
of grief, the frightening physical manifestations that tell us that something
is *grievously* wrong, the evidence that life has dealt us a mortal blow.
Experts have described the common characteristics of grief, but as any
bereaved person will attest, "You have to have been there to know what
it's like." One needs so much more than words to describe the first
terrible symptoms. There's that word again — *symptoms* — yet grief is not
a disease. One is not sick, though there are physical complaints that are
similar to those caused by illness. One is merely sick to the soul, as
someone has said.

Death is a psychological event that affects us physically. We can only
anticipate our own death; once it has happened, we're not around to
react to it. We can see someone else die and can react before (if there's
time) and after the fact, and oh, the reaction! The psychic pain comes
later, part of the long-term grieving process, and it must be faced, step
by agonizing step. But first there is this physical malaise, a euphemism for
the gut-tearing pain it involves. To describe the "symptoms," therefore,
requires detachment, and perhaps the indifference of one who does not
suffer. ("Tell me, Mrs. Lincoln, when did you first start having these
dreams about actors?").

My view is that all change involves some kind of loss and that the assimilation of loss involves grief. My consideration of the symptoms of grief must, then, include reactions both large and small, responses both dramatic and un-, but primarily in the first phase when they are essentially physical ones. As I appraise the effects of death and the subsequent changes it causes, I will try to refine and identify individual responses.

In the case of a severe loss, that is, death of a spouse or of a significant relationship, the physical, overt symptoms are easy to identify and universal: inability to eat, to sleep, to concentrate; visual and aural hallucinations; short attention span; general nervous tension; and, of course, tears — if one is lucky.

It is one of life's ironies for most women that they lose unwanted weight following bereavement or divorce without even trying. The pounds melt away, gone with the appetite. Who can eat when the throat is closed tight with fear and the stomach churning sick with tension? As a matter of fact, some people can. There are people who react to anxiety, fear, or stress by eating, stuffing themselves, in fact, as if to create a bulwark between them and pain, or to give their mouths something to "chew on" even as their minds try to digest what has happened. It's hard to generalize about eating patterns; one has only one's empirical observations to go on. My question about who can eat was based on my own tight throat and agitated stomach, no one else's. Unfair. I want to say that except for compulsive eaters who consume for comfort, most victims — for that is what one feels like, a victim — have no care or thought for food, but I'm wrong. Those who turn to food for solace will give me an argument.

What about sleep? Again I want to say that most people have difficulty sleeping following the death of a loved one, but what if one is a narcoleptic and sleeps under stress? Who will watch for me if I sleep, I want to ask, but perhaps others don't feel that way.

Anyone who has ever suffered the loss of a loved one needs no reminders of what it feels like in the first harrowing moments, hours, and days following bereavement. The first symptoms of grief are blatantly physical and destructive. In the case of a sudden death, equal parts awe, horror, and fear mingle to form an almost unbearable tension in the body and mind of the survivor. Sometimes it *is* unbearable and it takes a physical toll. In the case of a long terminal illness, the survivor, who has probably also been the caregiver, is usually physically and emotionally exhausted to the point that the first few hours following the actual death take on the weird contours of a twilight zone in terms of time and space. Few people retain any accurate or detailed memory of the first twenty-four hours after the death has occurred. The brain releases some sort of sedative that blessedly acts like a memory-wipe.

I'll go into the psychological stages in detail in the next chapter, but I rank suicide as one of the symptoms of grief, not tied to any one stage. The suicide rate in the first year following bereavement is four times as high among widowers as it is among the normal male population; in the second year, it's higher for widows. Rates of admission to hospital and the number of visits to their physicians is four or five times higher among widows in their first year of bereavement than among the general female population, while a sharp increase in stress-related diseases, such as heart attacks and strokes, is noted among recent widowers.

Adults are not the only ones to suffer during bereavement. Children exhibit many of the same effects, with loss of appetite and disturbed sleep patterns, including nightmares, indicating their daytime fears. Children either become very, very good — frighteningly so — or else act out. They can isolate themselves, withdrawing almost totally from human contact, or they can cling to a caregiver like a growth or an extra appendage. As with adults, any or all of this behavior is normal.

Nothing feels normal. Most survivors have the feeling that they are going insane. One of the first reassurances they need is that they are not, in fact, mad. People cope the way they have to, the way they have learned to, the way they've been accustomed to. One's conduct might be predicted from previous coping mechanisms. Death does not suddenly change one's behavior; it merely exaggerates it. There are as many different ways to react as there are people to react, but general patterns emerge, following very closely the patterns a person has already established. Some people go to pieces in times of crisis; others take on an unnatural calm and save the breakdown for later. Some people play a combination of sour grapes and Pollyanna ("I didn't really want to be a mother, anyway"; "It's really all for the best, we never got along"; "He would have been a vegetable"; "At least she was spared the pain"; and so on). Some people blame themselves; some people blame others. Some people hide from the world; others want to be surrounded by people and noise to keep them from their thoughts. Whatever feels natural is right, for the moment. The significant changes come later.

What is clear is perceived only in retrospect. By this event the world, that is, the world of the survivor, is divided into Before and After, Then and Now, but we don't know it yet. That was then, this is now.

In the meantime, right now, all the good advice that has ever been given is still appropriate. The physical body requires tender loving care, no more sudden changes, no shocks, if they can be avoided. Mild, bland, nutritious food, enough bedrest, if not sleep, enough exercise to encourage sleep but not to exhaust an already depleted body — in short, all the usual physical treatment for any shock should be applied to a bereaved survivor. The future is later. The grieving to come is very hard work.

7. The Stages of Grief

The heart itself cannot decide that the loss of a loved one is too much
for it; the liver alone does not see the shame of embarrassment;
the immune system does not know whether its client
is employed or not, divorced or not.
— ROBERT ORNSTEIN

THE FACTS OF LOSS ARE THE FACTS OF LIFE. ESSENTIALLY, change is what we all have to adjust to and absorb into our lives. In order to go on, we have to adjust to change and set up new patterns of behavior. For some, the adjustment period may not seem to take too long; for others it seems an eternity, and is hell on earth. ("Why this is hell," said Marlowe's Mephistopheles, "nor am I out of it.") The length of time required can be a few weeks, a year, two years, five, forever. No one really "gets over" a loss. No one can go back in time and recover what was there. One can only go forward, limping, wounded, staggering, proudly, humiliated, triumphant, determined, cheerful, resigned — it depends on the character, age, attitude, and faith of the survivor, and to some extent on the support system (but less, I think, than is popularly supposed).

The stages of this grief process can be monitored. There are recognizable steps along the way, common enough that they may be identified and labeled. Elisabeth Kübler-Ross is most noted for her catalog of the stages of grief she identified among the terminally ill. These relate closely to the stages a bereaved person goes through following the death of a loved one. Other doctors, psychologists, psychiatrists, and social workers working with the bereaved have refined or shifted slightly or added to the list, but the initial course of emotion is the same and is evident also among people who have suffered remoter deaths and the death of a relationship (divorce), as well as other losses.

The stages are: shock, denial, anger, bargaining, depression, and acceptance. These steps are most closely associated with the dying — those who know they are dying. For those who suffer after the fact of death, that is, the bereaved, there are variations on the theme.

Shock is self-explanatory. The same recoil that follows a physical blow affects the emotional circuits in the same way. It took people a long time to realize that some treatment was necessary for an emotional wound. After the First World War, veterans who hadn't been physically wounded were labeled "shell-shocked," but given little treatment of any kind, or tolerance. They were probably told, as victims of what was perceived as self-indulgent or prolonged grief, to "snap out of it." How?

The St. John's Ambulance First Aid course has taught thousands of people how to treat physical shock after a car crash or an accident: do not move the victim, wrap in blankets, keep warm, and so on. People have been realizing belatedly that the same treatment — TLC — works for emotional shock. I wish I had a nickel for every electric blanket I've recommended to the recently bereaved. I tell every widow and widower to warm the bed ahead of time, then to creep into the warmth and huddle.

Shock anesthetizes physical pain for a while; it has the same effect on the emotions. This fact explains the dry-eyed poise of widow or widower at the funeral and during the days immediately following. The recently bereaved are not controlled; they are numb. Later, pain strikes like a tidal wave with the first inexorable roll of consciousness and the accompanying cries of pain and bewilderment and fear:

- "How can I go on?"
- "Why me?"
- "My God, my God, why hast thou forsaken me?"

The waking coma of the immediately bereaved fools others into making assumptions about their consciousness and competence. Early on, within the first week of my husband's death, I didn't misunderstand what was being said to me so much as simply not register what our lawyer and insurance agent carefully spelled out for me. I was about as lively and sentient as a dish of yogurt, less so, actually, because yogurt is a bacteria, a living organism, and I wasn't. On the one hand, people assume some awareness on the part of the bereaved; on the other, they mistakenly seek to spare him or her.

The body must be seen. A stillborn baby must be rocked, a child should be held, a suicide must be acknowledged, an accident victim needs to be identified — all by the closest kin. Only by confronting reality can the bereaved begin to absorb it. My older son cried once — at least, in my presence — and that was when he saw his father in the coffin. It had to be. Bodies that are lost at sea or in deep lakes or on tall mountains; drowned or scattered or burned among wreckage; buried in unknown, distant graves; or vanished, fate unknown — such bodies, such deaths, never acquire any reality or immediacy for the bereaved. Their memory fades like an old Polaroid photograph; but is still there somehow, impossible to grieve fully. Neither their names nor their spirits are laid to rest because they are still partly present, almost alive, simply distant, but not departed. The second stage of grief, denial, becomes permanent, and the bereaved will stay in that nether world forever.

Denial in its own time is not all bad, if there is an end to it in sight. Denial should not go on indefinitely, but neither should it be cut off. To deny a death or a loss is to deny change and, ultimately, to deny the significance of what has happened. People do and say the strangest things in denial.

"You're kidding!" That's what one person said to me when I told her my husband had died. One doesn't kid about death; everyone knows that. Kidding was not my intent; my listener knew that. Her reaction was simply denial: it can't be true, therefore it's a joke, right? Wrong.

- "I can't believe it, I just can't believe it."
- "He was here a week ago, yesterday, an hour ago. How could he be gone now?"
- "But she looked so well. I thought she was getting better."
- "We were planning to go on a trip together. How could she go without me?"
- "But the operation was a success. How can he be dead?"
- "He's too young, just a little boy."
- "She never saw her new grandchild. She wanted to stay for its birth — she promised."
- "He was always such a careful driver, he couldn't have crashed."

- "I never told her how much I love her — she can't go until she knows."

On and on, the cries of denial, the disbelief, the negatives, the complaints: too soon, not yet, why now? why me? The cries are selfish. What they are is the first expression of self, the self that refuses to be buried with the dead. That's a good sign.

In *Future Shock*, Alvin Toffler describes four different denial responses to "high-speed change." All these "denier's strategies" are apparent in the reactions of the recently bereaved. I'll take Toffler's list of denial strategies and illustrate them with typical bereavement responses.

1. Outright denial

An initial attempt to block out reality is the most immediate, natural response to any disaster. The mind needs time to absorb stunning change; denial supplies that time. The blocking is simply closing compartments of understanding until the bad news can be assimilated. Only if such denial continues does it become dangerous to the denier. Similarly, anyone who pretends/denies that anything bad has happened in the face of incontrovertible evidence teeters on the edge of insanity. Think of King Lear who has carried Cordelia's body but who tries to believe she is still breathing: "This feather stirs: she lives!" . . . and then: "Do you see this? Look on her, — look, — her lips, — /Look there, look there! — " And he dies. (KING LEAR, V, III)

2. Specialism

This behavior confuses the observer. The bereaved person seems to be coping quite well, making the right noises and the right moves, but only in the mechanical aspects of life: carrying on at work, coping with the children, whatever has to be done. The emotions, however, have gone on hold. Questioned, the person will deny any trouble or particular pain. This performance is known as arrested grief, seen frequently in a teenager who grows up overnight and who becomes the confidant and support of the bereaved parent, allowing or being allowed no acknowledgment of, or time for, personal grieving, or in the bereaved parent who refuses to mention the name of a child who has died and who gets rid of all traces and mementoes, carrying denial to the point of eradicating the child's existence.

3. Obsessive reversion to previously successful adaptive routines
This behavior is more common before the death, being some kind of
fantasy to prevent the undesirable event from occurring. If we eat our
vegetables/get more rest/take a holiday/confess our sins, everything will
be all right. If we stop fighting/go home/attend church regularly, nothing
bad will ever happen. Old solutions do not work with new problems,
however, especially when the problem is irrevocable.

4. Super simplifier
One universal answer will wipe away the pain. I call this the "Band-Aid
Solution." It simply doesn't work with one of the most traumatic psychic
wounds a human being can receive. There is no instant cure, immediate
solace, or fast-fast-fast relief. Others are more likely to impose the Band-
Aid Solution upon the bereaved than are the bereaved to adopt it as their
own denial mechanism.

Denial, as I have said, is not all bad. Psychologists Robert Ornstein and
David Sobel claim that denial has received bad press, that it has been
perceived as entirely negative, causing pathological consequences. Sometimes, they say, "we need our illusions."

A parable: This was a story I saw on TV years ago, and I don't know
who wrote it, about four men in a public hospital ward. One of the men
has the bed by the window and when the shade is raised each morning
he describes the weather and the changing scene below: a light breeze in
the leaves of the trees in the park across the street causes dancing shadows
on the flowerbeds, a nursemaid pushes a baby carriage and flirts with a
hotdog vendor on the corner, and so on. When the Window Patient is
taken away for extensive tests, the others begin to grumble. Why should
he have exclusive rights to the window? Maybe there are other sights he
doesn't tell them about. They persuade the nurse to shift one of their
number to the vacant bed. This man settles eagerly and peers out the
window. . . . "Oh no!" he exclaims. The view is of a brick wall. The
window opens on an airshaft of the building.

Quickly the men persuade the nurse to restore the status quo and
leave the window bed vacant as before, awaiting the return of their
roommate. When he returns, they can't wait for him to settle and to
look out the window and tell them what he sees:

"Well," he says, "the late afternoon sun is slanting over the play-ground area, and two of the cutest little kids you ever saw are bouncing on the seesaw. . . ."

The other men listen, and smile.

Sometimes, indeed, we need our illusions. A person can take just so much reality at a time. Self-deception drapes a veil across our eyes and shields us from reality until we are ready to bear it. "Happiness," wrote Jonathan Swift in the eighteenth century, "is a state of being well deceived." Psychologist Richard Lazarus says that we all "pilot our lives in part by illusions and by self-deceptions that give meaning and substance to life."

There are dangers, of course, in unrealistic denial. The overweight person is foolish to ignore a pain in his left arm and go bowling. However, after the heart attack (if they survive it) or the diagnosis of disease, deniers seem to have a better chance of recovery if they refuse to think they're dying or if they deny the evidence of disease and fight it. Denial is a kind of hope, a refusal to accept the bad news of illness or impending death. And after death (or divorce or any traumatic Life Event) has seemingly removed all hope, denial provides a glimmer of control in a world that seems to have lost sense.

Denial is pretence, the best there is. Deep down, in the center core, truth resides. Most people hide from it, pretend it doesn't exist, deny they know what's going on, until the facts seep out, little by little, from self to the outside world. Conversely, if the self has been sucked out over the years, if it has been invested (immured?) in a marriage, a child, a career, a way of life, and suddenly its resting place is withdrawn, then, again little by little, it has to be recovered and tucked back into its core. Ultimately, the entire grieving process is a recovery of self. In the meantime, denial goes on:

- "I'm fine, don't worry about me."
- "Life is a cabaret, my friend."
- "I'm alive, aren't I?"

As denial sinks slowly in the west, the red tide of anger rises. Such a madness, but such a powerful defense, is this next fortress after denial in the preservation of the self. Anger asserts the I who is angry and predicates the word, circumstances, fate, people, the God one is angry with. So far, we have not been allowed much anger in the face of death.

Anger is not "nice." Nice people don't get angry. Friends, relatives, helpers are doing the best they can. It's not anyone's fault if someone died (and, if it is, that can be resolved and compensated by a malpractice suit or a damages case), or if the marriage broke up, or the house burned down, or the job slipped away. That's just the way things worked out. No use crying over spilled milk. Don't blame me — or anyone.

A lot of people do blame God, who had nothing to do with it. "God is subtle," said Einstein, "but not malicious." If the immutable laws of the universe have been defied, someone is bound to be hurt. The law of gravity leads us to expect that an object falling from a great-enough height will be broken. It is the nature of cancer cells to destroy healthy ones. Guns fired at human flesh damage it, often fatally. These are statements of fact and have nothing to do with God's mysterious ways. God does not cause or will bad things to happen. However, when bad things happen, God, properly sought and however defined, will grant the strength and wisdom to survive. Anger with God simply delays the process. As for those who do not put a name to an all-knowing Consciousness, whether benign or not, the most comforting thing I can say is that it ain't over till it's over. The same laws of cause and effect apply no matter how they were established, or by Whom.

Legitimate anger signals discomfort, resentment, displeasure with the way things are. Anger demands change. Regrettably, people don't get angry often enough, or not enough to do anyone any good, least of all the angry one. Women, particularly, expect to bear up and carry on under any circumstances; they are not permitted to get angry, as men are not permitted to cry. Women have to be ladylike. Men are not exempt; they are expected to control their violent feelings and to behave themselves. No one is allowed to stamp her feet or shake his fist. Even venting anger, if done ineffectively, serves no useful purpose. Properly used and directed, anger can supply energy to change the situation that has caused the anger, or if it cannot be changed (death is sort of irrevocable), then anger can be refocused so that expectations can be changed. *Focus* is the key word.

The bereaved are angry, frequently at the departed for leaving them (even if it was not their intention or fault), often at society for ignoring them (society doesn't know what to do any more, with the old rules of mourning and respect in such disrepair), and usually at themselves for not being able to cope with the crisis. Silent submission never did anyone much good, except saints, and look how long it takes to be canonized these days. Better to be noisy.

> Do not go gentle into that good night
> Rage, rage against the dying of the light.
> —DYLAN THOMAS, *THE POEMS*

After the fact as well, anger's clarity can be used to define the self that's been denied and anger's white light can illuminate the tattered remnants of life so that they may be mended.

The bargaining and depression that Kübler-Ross has described in the terminally ill and dying are not expressed in the same way among the bereaved. It's too late for the bereaved to bargain; they slip into depression instead. Depression is a form of anger, which continues because the untenable circumstances continue. Depression is triggered by the lack of control resulting from loss, the feeling that one's life and the conduct thereof are out of one's hands, that everyone is a pawn of Fate.

What's the use? What can I do about it? How can I change events? What good will anything do? Who cares what happens to me? How will I survive? Like worried rats in a maze, our thoughts run into dead ends wherever they turn. The hopelessness of the situation seems to emphasize one's own helplessness in the face of it, and leads to depression with its feelings of low self-esteem, self-recrimination (whose fault is it?), and self-hatred. The old self that got lost emerges with all kinds of hyphens attached to it. The one that's missing is self-discipline.

And so we come to acceptance. For those who are facing death, acceptance is a kind of triumphant acquiescence. It's a hygienic high, not granted to everyone, this right, good way of dying. This almost eager acceptance can occur only in a certain kind of death and with a certain kind of person.

What about my husband who dropped dead and never knew what hit him? No time for acceptance there. What about accident victims, and flood and fire and famine and earthquake victims? What about people who leave their minds long before their bodies are ready to go? No time for acceptance, or no sense in it, in those cases. And what about people who aren't talkers? I don't mean the ones who are angry or frightened and who say they don't want to talk about their illness or their impending death; they eventually open up and feel better for giving words to their fears and for saying goodbye. But there are genuinely inarticulate people whose very soul shrivels at the thought of giving sorrow words. They have lived and loved by showing, not telling, and they're determined to die the same way. I say let them.

I said goodbye to one of those people recently, one of nature's noblemen, as reserved in his death as he had been in his life. Though he went through a crash course of shock, denial, anger, bargaining, and depression (he died very quickly, in about four months), his final acknowledgment of his unavoidable exit was tacit and nonverbal. I told him I was writing a book about grieving. "Give it to my wife," he said. I will.

For the living, grief has various other manifestations, defined by writers other than Kübler-Ross. Peter Marris, for example, in his book *Loss and Change*, reporting on his sociological and psychological researches into the effects of major changes in people's lives, summarizes the grief transition (Kübler-Ross's stages) as progressing from "shock to acute distress to re-integration." (Hold that word *re-integration*.) Therapist Lily Pincus, in her book *Death and the Family*, identifies the grief responses as shock (and fear), followed by "a controlled phase" during which the mechanics have to be dealt with — that is, the funeral, the people, the financial arrangements, and so on.

Searching follows, according to Pincus, an almost automatic defense against acceptance of loss. This corresponds somewhat to the denial stage in Kübler-Ross's rundown, that is, to the inability to accept reality. Marris refers to this stage as a "search for continuity," and many people can identify with it. It accounts for Queen Victoria's standing order for that memorial bedroom she refused to change. It accounts for any number of people playing favorite music, looking at old pictures, and going back to scenes of former happiness: a favorite restaurant, vacation spot, city. Somehow the pain of the contrast between happy then and miserable now is balanced by sweet memory.

I found myself doing more than making visits to old haunts. For over a year, and not entirely consciously, I attempted to carry out some of our future plans. I managed to get to cities to see people we had been hoping to visit and to take in events we had planned to attend. A friend pointed out to me that I was being morbid, wallowing in such might-have-beens.

Twelve years elapsed before I was back in London, England, one of our favorite cities, without Bill. I set about getting theater tickets and necessarily walking in familiar streets, doing things we loved to do: eating a pub lunch, having tea at Fortnum & Mason, and, of course, going to the theater. After the first day of too much walking, I caught a cab back to my hotel. As I crossed by Trafalgar Square, I could see us in my mind's eye, on our first trip, sitting on a stone bench over there, beyond the fountain, drinking an orange squash, poring over a map as we rested our aching feet and decided where to go next. This older, solitary woman in the cab began to cry, no sentimental moistening of the eye but big, wet, splotchy tears pouring down my face in great buckets of self-pity. The poor cab driver didn't know what to do.

Love, so all the experts say, does not explain grief (though it seems to exacerbate it). Loss does not involve merely (!) the loss of a loved one. It includes far more: the loss of a job, role, setting, past, present, future. When one grieves over a loss, one is grieving the loss of self, that part of the self that will never be the same again, that can never be recovered. That is the fact, the lesson, that has to be learned, over and over again.

Thus we begin to understand Lily Pincus when she states that searching is the "principal behavior pattern evoked by loss." Searching is evident in the absence of mind in unguarded moments early on that takes us into old paths; it's present in the hallucinations, projections of mind, involving phantom sights and sounds; it's encouraged in the conscious trips down memory lane, reminiscing, recalling times past; and it's involuntary in the dreaming, as we attempt to integrate external fact with internal desire. The dreams are painful, but benign, somehow benign, I am sure.

I call them "teaching dreams." Most people experience them after the death of a loved one. It's as if the subconscious mind has been enlisted to help the psyche assimilate the fact of death. Always in my dreams, my husband and I have been separated geographically or are emotionally estranged. If we see each other, we get along very well but he refuses to stay with me, and I end up begging him to return to me.

"We get along so well," I remember pleading with him in the first such dream. "Don't you think, if we tried, we could get together again— oh, no!" I broke off in pain. "I keep forgetting—you're dead!" I had to keep remembering that; I had to be reminded over and over again. It takes a while for the subconscious to absorb the fact.

In another early, vivid dream, I was in a very large building, some sort of a hotel. I was on the level of the public rooms, with crowds of people, none of whom I had anything to do with, or they with me. All the rooms were white, white-on-white. I searched through them — ballrooms, convention and meeting rooms, dining rooms, even a gym (all white), looking for an elevator or stairs to take me up to a higher level. I was going to meet my husband who was on an upper floor, but I couldn't find a way off the floor I was trapped on. No way out, no way up, no way to join him.

Searching, whatever form or path it takes, may lead to various discoveries, the most desirable one being some sense of the loved one's continuing presence. This sense is not a projection, a memory, or a dream, but rather an internalization of the lost object or person.

> At first when you left
>> there was a white space like a blank
>
> Then the white space moved inside
>> no bigger than a moth, testing
>> wings against walls
>
> It has taken longer to grow you than a child
>
> Never to be delivered

Once established, in context, as it were, the internalization provides continuity. The link with the past is set in place, strong enough to provide connections with the future. Such a chain of continuity takes time to be forged, and there will be relapses, breaks in the chain (weak links) that leave one directionless and foundering. It's more than memory I'm talking about. It's the certain, comforting knowledge that what was once possessed cannot be removed. And so I refer to My Other Life with a kind of humor but a confidence in its validity in my past. And when I see young love (or old love), I just have to remind myself that I had it once too, a good one. It helps, a little, and softens the edges of pain.

Anger and hostility are stages recognized by Pincus as well as by

Kübler-Ross and these, painful as they are, supply the iron in one's soul. For, in order to internalize the lost person or thing, one requires recognition. Internalization does not entail idealization. The person (or thing) has to be seen clearly, warts and all, hence the anger and hostility — *hygienic* anger, *healthy* hostility.

Widows, more frequently than widowers, have been accused of putting their late husbands on a pedestal, but widowers do it too. It's very hard to live with; too reverent an attitude toward the dead kills the living. No present event, no child of the deceased, no subsequent mate of the widowed, can hold a candle to the idealized memory of the departed, not even a memorial candle. It's a no-win situation. A little anger and hostility help to smash the pedestal and bring the human being down from the misty view of idealization and the haze of illusion into clear 20:20 perception.

No rose-colored hindsight glasses for me. My husband was an earthy man, with a great sense of humor, and totally human. (I still think I'm not as nice a person as he was, but that's my problem.) I miss the whole man, not an idealized creation. I do sometimes wonder whether we would still be married if he were alive today, considering how I have changed. Presumably we would have changed together.

Anger and hostility are directed not only at the departed (how dare they leave?), but also at other people: the doctors who should have known more, the nurses who should have done more, the careless motorist who should have been more careful, our friends and neighbors who should have been more thoughtful, and almost everyone else who will insist on continuing to live as if nothing had happened. Everyone is at fault, including the departed. How is it possible to grieve for such an imperfect human being, to crave to be whole when even the restoration of the person would not make us whole? We long for what we loved, we shudder and feel guilty for recoiling from what we hated. We feel anger at ourselves, we hate ourselves too, we see ourselves too clearly with that odious perfect sight. If this sounds confused and inconsistent, it is. We are deep into ambivalence.

Pincus and Marris both list ambivalence as a significant stage of grief. We've already experienced mixed feelings, but ambivalence is more than that. Ambivalence is wanting to die too and yet (slowly) recovering former eating and sleeping habits and driving carefully and not taking unnecessary risks; ambivalence is never wanting anyone or -thing to replace what was lost, but unaccountably responding with the flesh (if not with the mind or heart) to a lusty pass, or actually wanting to buy (or even buying) something frivolous and unnecessary to life support, such as clothes, a painting, a game(!), or the first asparagus in spring. Such betrayal!

Ambivalence is remembering one's own less-than-perfect behavior toward the departed: harsh words spoken, good deeds left undone, a lack of cooperation, a critical attitude, neglect, anger, less-than-perfect love, at the same time as one remembers similar commissions and omissions on the side of the departed. Not everyone will agree, but I think more ambivalence goes into the reaction to the death of a parent than of a mate. No matter what our chronological age, we retain a push-me-pull-you attitude to our parents: fierce independence and resentment at perceived interference pitted against the demand for unconditional love and what we owe forever for the mere fact of life. Ambivalence indeed!

Ambivalence goes hand-over-mouth with guilt. Guilt is saying you're sorry; love is forgiving. Guilt is predicated on love, and sorry is implicit. But when the beloved's voice is silent and can no longer utter forgiveness, who will forgive us? So the guilt goes on, unassuaged and often confused.

Another parable: a little kid is sitting on his front steps, looking at all his friends going to school. "Ha ha," he shouts at them. "I don't have to go to school today. Ha ha, my uncle died!"

Therein lies the confusion. No matter who dies, *I'm alive!* Is that triumph, or what? Guilt seems to be written in stone.

> *The Moving Finger writes; and, having writ,*
> *Moves on: nor all your Piety nor Wit*
> *Shall lure it back to cancel half a Line,*
> *Nor all your Tears wash out a Word of it.*
> —EDWARD FITZGERALD, *THE RUBÁIYÁT OF OMAR KHAYYÁM*

Some people try to wipe out guilt. They raise monuments to the dead, not only mausoleums but memorial gifts and posthumous tokens of esteem to ease the burden of guilt. Overcompensation does not equal expiation.

Sometimes, after idealization and compensation, comes a funny kind of identification. This is one wrinkle that no one even hints at. A woman will wear a favorite sweater of her husband's, or wrap herself in his dressing gown to sleep in, or use his golf clubs or pen (I wore my husband's colorful bikini underwear — kinky!). A man will learn to cook, including cakes and bread, emulating his wife's prowess in the kitchen, and one widower reported that he did what George Burns said he did after Gracie Allen died — moved into his wife's bed. Either spouse might become wittier, to be like the one who left.

Bill and I used to send witty telegrams to the company on opening nights (my husband was manager of the Stratford Festival at the time of his death). On the opening night of Turgenev's *A Month in the Country*, about three months after Bill's death, I sat down — consciously — with him to devise a message for the wire. "A month in the country," I wrote, "is worth two in the bush." It's a good line, but which of us thought of it? I have been told many times since Bill's death what a witty woman I am. Has my husband become a ventriloquist and I his dummy, or is this identification? Freud says, "If one has lost an object or has to give it up, one often compensates oneself by identifying oneself with it." Bill was a very funny man and now I am a funny woman.

All these various stages are not carried out in orderly progression, as on a gameboard. If the steps resemble those of any game, it's Snakes and Ladders, in which a slow, step-by-step advance can be wiped out by a sickening slide down a snake. On the other hand, there are always those ladders. Anger, hostility, guilt, compensation, and idealization are all stops on the way, but not rest-stops and not full ones. We go on. . . .

The snakes represent *regression*, and how horrible it is. When a grieving person hits the snakes, that's when insanity threatens — the snake pit? Grieving is a grievous mental wound — *not* a disease — a bleeding, quivering hole in the psyche. Childish behavior, paralyzing terror, irrational actions, wild swings of emotion, and deadly apathy — all characterize the griever at the very same time as the same person may exhibit exceptional self-discipline, remarkable maturity, and even some wryly humorous insights into the situation.

Right after the funeral service, the children and I got into the car behind the hearse — one can't get much closer and not be dead oneself — and waited for the cortege to the cemetery. People had to walk by our car on the way to the parking lot, and we were careful not to meet any glances. But what does one talk about in that car at that time?

My son John (then aged fourteen) said, "Did you see Uncle Jack? He made a dart out of the order of service." My lips twitched. "Your father would think that was very funny," I said. "Can you hear him? He'd be asking, 'Who invited him?' "

We started to laugh, I mean wild laughter — more like hysteria. We shook with laughter and had to cover our faces and mouths so that the people coming out of the church would not see us laughing. I have never been so grateful for laughter in my life.

The humor is wry and its occasions far between. The irrationality bordering on insanity is what terrifies the bereaved. They have terrible questions to ask and no one seems able to answer them:

- "Am I going crazy?"
- "How am I going to go on?"
- "Will I ever regain control of my life?"

These are horrible but normal steps toward recovery. The old electric blanket (or duvet) that was such a help during the first sleepless nights still comes in handy. It creates the closest thing to a womb we can manage. A warm bed after a pampering soak in a warm bath (with Epsom salts, not bubbles) is very therapeutic.

All these "steps" are nothing so definitive; they are phases the bereaved slip in and out of, often to the dismay of their friends, who want them to "get on with it." Continuing grief gets to be a bore, to say the least. Just when the sufferer most needs understanding, sympathy, acceptance, forgiveness, support, and above all patience, that's when people are least likely to offer any of them. Survivors say so regularly and so similarly that they might be reading from a single script: "You find out who your friends are." What they mean is they have discovered who among their friends keep hanging around, offering a shoulder, an ear, a drink, continuing sympathy and endless patience — all without judging or lecturing. This is not a time when anyone wants to hear "You should be doing this"; "You shouldn't be doing that"; "You should snap out of it."

Snapping out of it is not the way. I have compared grief to muscle spasms: the pain must not be resisted; it must be confronted and passed through — clear to the other side. The other side is what Kübler-Ross calls

66

acceptance, Pincus adaptation, and Marris re-integration. Acceptance is not a passive state, and it is never reached by simple acquiescence. Kübler-Ross describes some moving scenes when patients of hers accepted their imminent death, the final step. For the bereaved, the step is neither final nor singular. It happens over and over again. One keeps renegotiating peace.

A parable (or maybe just a simile): loss is like a huge rock dropped into the middle of a lake. The water boils around the intrusion and rolls out in waves from the central disturbance. A boat moored at a dock on shore begins to rise and fall with the incoming waves and bumps repeatedly against the dock. It keeps on bumping, rising and falling, and bumping, more and more gently as the water smooths and recovers its serenity. Another passing boat causes more ripples and waves. The rising and the falling and the bumping begin again.

Finally, people start saying, "Well, so-and-so seems to be getting over it" — whatever it is, usually a death, often a divorce. Appearances are deceiving; assumptions are just plain wrong. One does not "get over" a loss, as one gets over measles or a bad haircut. Loss is permanent. Grief is a wound, a mental wound that develops scar tissue around and over it so that "normal" behavior and activity are possible, but it's still there. So many people do not understand this simple, painful fact.

Once acknowledged and absorbed, this truth indeed enables the bereaved to go on, poorer for the loss but richer in spirit, fuller because emptier.

> The deeper that sorrow carves into your being, the more joy you can contain.
> — KAHLIL GIBRAN, THE PROPHET

No one talks about compassion. Compassion is a learned attribute and begets a deftness of its own. Words from the Universal Script: "You have to have been there," says many a widow about the astonishing pain and fear she has discovered. "It takes one to know one," say the widowers more gruffly, as they discuss the lack of sex and social life to explain their commitment to ballgames and booze. All these truisms indicate that compassion rises out of intimate association with similar experience. Compassion explains the reason for all the support groups springing up around the country, and for their success. Most people, once they have stumbled upon pain, feel compelled to reach out a hand to steady others on the path and to support them over the rough spots they have already traversed.

A warning: sometimes compassion can go too far. Sometimes it can lead to exploitation, as one widow explicitly warned me in a letter: "As to doing something for someone else, it seemed that was all I ever did. When it was not my own children or the PTA or the church or a neighbor in need, it was the house needing repair or attention. There is, of course, validity in the statement that doing for others helps us to forget ourselves, but sometimes I used to go on my self-pity binges and think, 'If I'm supposed to always be helping others, why is no one supposed to help me?' I got so uptight one time I decided I would have engraved on my tombstone 'I trusted in God and look where it got me.' "

Withdrawal as a symptom of grief appears to have been overlooked in the stages outlined by various experts. Such withdrawal, a retreat into oneself, is most evident in parents who are losing or have lost a child. It sometimes occurs to the point that each parent, having the corner on grief, attempts to reject the other. Each also seems to find it difficult to acknowledge the existence of any other children they might have. We'll deal with that reaction in more detail later.

The cave instinct must still lurk in each of us, and something of the primitive animal. Deeply wounded, human beings exhibit this basic need to lick their wounds in private and, conversely, to simulate health and strength in public. A bold front of invulnerability protects them from further attack — but how lonely and frightening self-imposed isolation can be! If the instinct to withdraw continues, it ceases to be self-protecting and becomes self-defeating.

The reasoning is clear: "If I don't care, if I don't let anyone or anything touch me deeply again, then I can't be hurt again." Examples abound of such withdrawal behavior. It happens a lot among widows who have nursed a mate through a long, drawn-out terminal illness, or lost a husband to a sudden, unexpected death. The former simply cannot face the pain and fatigue and the long farewell of the slow death of a loved one; the latter hate the thought of having the carpet pulled out from under them again, leaving them gasping in shock and terror.

I fell into the latter category. It seems, as I look back now, that I saw to it that any eligible man who came too near did not get too near.

I discovered that I was at my best in relationships with men who lived in other area codes. I think my reasons were not as self-defeating as they are for people who deny the core of their being. I simply (and unconsciously) made other choices. I still try to remain open. People who choose not to choose anything shut down. The fear of another devastating bereavement has deadened their lives.

It's a very real fear. I met one woman who has lost four husbands — the first to divorce, and three to death. I became acquainted with her shortly before her fourth marriage. When I learned of her bereavement only seven months later, I burst out, "How can you bear it? So many losses!"

"I can't," she said, "but my fourth marriage was the happiest of all, and I wouldn't have missed it for anything."

Other women are less courageous. I heard of another widow who turned down the chance of a second marriage because of the apprehension that she might have to nurse another man to his grave. Ironically, she developed Alzheimer's disease and died, while her might-have-been second husband is still alive and well.

I joked in a speech once that, if I married again, it would be to a much younger man so he wouldn't die on me, and a woman came up to me afterwards to tell me that the same reasoning lay behind her second marriage to a younger man but that he now lay ill with an incurable, wasting disease that was turning him into an old man before her eyes. That blew that theory.

The moral to these stories is that evasion doesn't work. None of us can hide from life. As long as we're living, we have to keep doing so as fully and openly as we can. We must keep on seeing a new response worth making, a new commitment worth undertaking, and a new meaning worth acknowledging. Adapting to change is an integral part of consenting to it. Adaptation is even harder work than acceptance.

Think of Darwin's theory of the survival of the fittest. In order to survive, species adapt to their environment and develop according to the demands placed upon them. So, too, with any change or loss in our lives, we must adapt. The blind learn Braille; the deaf learn sign language. The amputee learns to walk again with the aid of a prosthesis. The paraplegic becomes a Man in Motion in a wheelchair. And the bereaved — who have lost not sight or hearing or mobility, but meaning — learn new purpose and see and hear and move in a different way. That's adaptation.

Adaptation at first involves a clinging to the past. After the isolation, after the searching, after the attempt to re-create what has disappeared and to carry on as if nothing had happened, after all that, comes the first tentative effort to try something new. The changes are gradual at first. I changed grocery stores because I couldn't stand meeting my husband's ghost charging me with his cart down every aisle. The dinner hour changed, along with the old timetable based on the schedule of someone who was no longer coming home. More sweeping changes followed, with subsequent adaptation. Now, so many years later, the changes are so vast that I refer to my other life in capitals: My Other Life. And the person who lived that life (me) was An Other Person. Now that Other Person can say lightheartedly, when a friend speaks of her fall preserves, "I used to make freezer strawberry jam in My Other Life," or "I used to make buckets of garlic dill pickles in My Other Life." I am eyed askance as if I had been reincarnated rather than simply adapted for another purpose.

What one does, finally, with all this adjustment and adaptation, is create a new self. An *Other* Person. Grief continues to be a creative process.

III

DEATH BE NOT PROUD

There are so many ways to die yet in the end
there isn't much to choose among them.
The gate is narrow.

8. Kinds of Death

No one has ever died who was ready to die.
—ANTIPHANES, *c.* 350 B.C.

THE FIRST ASSIGNMENT IN A COURSE ON DEATH AND DYING is a written composition: write your own obituary. This task accomplishes at least three objectives: one, it makes you face your own mortality; two, it makes you assess your life; three, it gives you a chance to think about how you would like (?) to die. Not many people get that opportunity, not even the ones who think they're doing it deliberately, that is, committing suicide.

There are a lot of ways to die, old ways and new ways. Until the Challenger explosion, the only person I ever heard of who died because he flew toward the sun was the mythical Daedalus. (His father, Icarus, glued wings to his shoulders but the fixative melted in the heat of the sun and the wingless wonder fell to earth.) People die under the ground as well as up in the sky, in cave-ins and mine explosions; they die under water, from drowning and from implosions in the lungs (the bends); they die from dirty needles as well as dirty water now, and from germs, bacteria, and viruses that we keep on finding new names for. We haven't mentioned murder. They had that then too. Man's inhumanity to man has gone on ever since Cain killed Abel.

Few infants die now from being "exposed"—left outside in a bowl on the hill above Athens because *she* was the wrong sex; or from being farmed out to a wet nurse, or even "laid on" in bed (a common cause of death listed in the Domesday Book).

Accidents, freak or otherwise, are the leading cause of death among young people, especially boys, from the ages of ten to twenty. Cars, boats, alcohol, drugs, and an overdeveloped sense of adventure can do just about anyone in with the right (or wrong) combination of circumstances and timing. Women, young or old, don't die as regularly as they used to in childbirth since doctors started washing their hands before a delivery. That simple procedure reduced maternal mortality by about a thousand percent and raised women's life expectancy by thirty-some years since the turn of this century. Heart attacks, strokes, cancer — these are the leading causes of death in North America as we head into the twenty-first century.

Our idealized pictures of death conjure up the peaceful, white-haired old lady, frail but in perfect health, gently rocking herself into her permanent sleep after her ninety-seventh birthday party when her entire family wished her well, or the steely, eighty-six-year-old man dropping dead after shoveling the snow off his front walk, or that mythical ninety-two-year-old rake being shot by a jealous husband. Of course, each of these scenarios happens so rarely, it's not idealized but extraordinary. People, old and young, just keep on dying. Our children die; our friends die; we also die. Parents, one or both, can die young, suddenly or slowly, leaving young children; or middle-aged, accidentally or on purpose; or faltering, losing their faculties before they leave their bodies; or suffering the destruction of their bodies while their bewildered spirits still deny death. Our life-companions die and leave us tottering at the edge of an abyss, swaying, praying to be able to go too. And then, finally, when it is time for us to leave, are we ever really prepared? Perhaps, if we're old or mature enough. There is no ideal way to go. As my late husband used to say, "One out of one dies of something."

I want to deal with the kinds of death we encounter before I go on to consider our relationships with those who die. Death is no respecter of age or position. We all know that. We have seen the recent, tragic, and multiplying deaths from the new epidemic of AIDS and the cruel judgment society places on those who suffer from it. We have seen murder slash across boundaries of age, gender, and role to overwhelm its survivors with anguished questions. Suicide destroys not only its perpetrator but the survivors, forever reproachful and guilty. Sudden death hurls trust in life out the window and leaves the survivors ambivalent about any secure future, while a slow, long-term death can almost kill the caregiver during the terminal illness. The kinds of death there are to die thus cut across our relationships with the dead. Such a wealth/dearth to choose from!

If we had to choose between a terminal illness and a sudden, unexpected death for our loved ones, we would probably choose the swift end for the sake of the one departing. Both exits are painful to those left to grieve, with only different emphases to choose between them, and no appreciable lightening of pain. In the case of a lengthy terminal illness, the caregiver runs a risk of illness after months, even years, of stress, poor sleep, weight loss, perhaps financial burdens, certainly physical ones — traveling to and from hospital or onerous home care, in addition to one's continuing, regular responsibilities — and deep concern for the pain and physical symptoms suffered by the loved one. The illness of a family member puts pressure on the family as a whole and shifts the relationships and responses of its members to each other. If the sick one is in the hospital for any length of time, home life is arrested. Meals are sketchy, and social life is nonexistent. Home becomes a jumping-off place while all the significant living goes on at the hospital. If home care is undertaken, the house acquires the febrile, urgent atmosphere of an emergency ward. Again, social life is nonexistent and the time frame of the entire household is based on the schedule of the sick one. Ironically, however, real time is suspended: there is no future now, none worth contemplating. As one caregiver said, "There is no forward to look to."

Anticipatory grief achieves this much: it says some of the goodbyes. Some financial preparations for the future can be made when/*if* (it depends on the amount of denial going on) the terminal illness is fully acknowledged, but anticipation — dread — of lifestyle changes seems to cause more anxiety than confidence. No one wants to think ahead to Christmas or travel or holidays without one's mate, and few people can face the thought of any drastic changes, such as moving from the home or even the city to something smaller, more convenient, less expensive, whatever. Why think about it? Maybe it won't happen. Denial, in fact, often stops any practical, detailed plans. All concerned find it easier to focus on the present, on the day-to-day, increasing trauma of an ongoing illness and the problems it continually presents. Both the sick one and the caregiver get caught in the physical trap of the disease, and spend their time coping with medication, food, and perhaps new treatments, instead of using the time to communicate with each other and to explore the meaning of their lives.

It is often hard or impossible for those facing death — their own or that of their loved ones — to talk about death. Some kind of mind-numbing anesthetic prevents any confrontation with the facts. This kind of denial is particularly hard on a dying child who knows that death is imminent but whose parents refuse to acknowledge the fact to themselves, thereby denying anyone a chance to be honest. Kübler-Ross tells story after story of people who finally broke down the barriers and talked to each other about what was uppermost in their minds. She says that this kind of breakthrough results in a tranquil acceptance of death and a peaceful farewell to loved ones. It's certainly more painful for the survivor if words unspoken and love unexpressed remain after the dialogue has been silenced.

But what if there is no time for words? Sudden death cuts off communication instantly. The long conversation is over and if there are things still unsaid, they remain so. "Nice" — if that's the word — for the one who left not to have suffered long or to have faced with increasing despair a physical deterioration from which there was no recovery, no cessation but death. Lights out, snapped off. The survivor, however, blinded by the sudden darkness, staggers with the shock and pain of that swift departure, with no preparation and no leave-taking. A sudden death usually happens to relatively younger people: accident, murder, heart attack, a quick killer disease, undetected, unexpected. My husband's freakish death by asphyxiation was perhaps triggered by a cardiac arrest. Whatever the cause, it was unexpected and he is gone. At forty-five, he had a heart too young to die. The point is that an early, unexpected death leaves one not only with the shock and terror and finality of death but also with a lot of living still to be done. Long-term plans are scrapped; speculations and projections are wiped away; hopes are blasted. Small wonder that the suddenly bereaved seldom wish to reinvest their lives in another marriage — too chancy.

Age, of course, is not a cause of death; life, as everyone says, is the biggest killer. We're all terminally ill, the cracker-barrel philosophers remind us; some of us are simply in longer remission than others. When people die at a very old age, there is usually no single cause of death. They simply slow down and wear out, as if their batteries have run dry. The hard part is that sometimes the wits run out before the power goes. A world statistic informs us that 10 percent of people over the age of sixty-five suffer from Alzheimer's or other forms of dementia.

It is said that Alzheimer's kills twice: first the mind, then the body. A person doesn't actually die of Alzheimer's. After a period of some five to ten years of steady deterioration, the organism thus weakened succumbs to pneumonia or some other disease. The symptoms of Alzheimer's are initially dismaying to the sufferer: memory loss, including language skills, impaired judgment, and a gradually increasing disorientation. The victim will become at first anxious, then irritated, then angry, then depressed, and then possibly so removed from normal thought processes that the disorientation, the shock and the pain, pass over to the caregiver. The patient is no longer the person the caregiver once knew and loved. Pearl Buck's husband declined and disappeared like that. Buck writes: "I do not know whether it is easier to have the end come suddenly or gradually over the years. I think, if I had been given the choice, I would have preferred a sudden end, shock and all. Then memory would not be entangled with the slow and agonizing fading of perception and speech and at last recognition of those loved and dear. There is, however, one balm. He did not know of his own decline."

We are familiar with the term *role reversal*, when the adult child must take over and care for the aging parent. In no case is this more poignant than with Alzheimer's. Here are some comments from adult children about their child-like parents:

- "Before, she had out-dazzled the sun; now, I was the one who brightened her day and made her laugh."
- "Sometimes I was angry at her for being so helpless and taking so long to die."
- "I drop my expectations and allow him the freedom to be old and confused."
- "I don't look forward to having to put him into a nursing home; in fact I pray that he'll die."

Canadian writer Donna Sinclair writes of an encephalitis victim who suffered the same mental deterioration and memory loss characteristic of Alzheimer's victims. The man's wife kept visiting him in the hospital until, one day, he told her she should stop.

"I don't think you should keep coming to see me," he said. "They tell me I am married."

"Yes," she explained gently. "You are married to me." He absorbed this fact slowly.

"Tell me," he asked. "Are we happy?"

Hear the heart break.

A new source of trenchant pain is being discovered with ever-increasing frequency by those with Acquired Immune Deficiency Syndrome (AIDS). At first mistakenly called the gay cancer, it has become one of the most terrifying and fastest-spreading diseases in North America. The rough estimates of the number of children who will die of it before the end of the century are going up all the time — ten thousand to twenty thousand at my last reading. The anger connected with AIDS is legitimate because of the lack of public support, sympathy, or understanding for PLWAs (Persons Living with AIDS).

Lovers are anything but blithe these days as they face the tragic, agonizing deaths of their companions and peers, with the added fear that they, too, may die of AIDS. Those who struggle with the terminal illness or sudden heart attack of their loved one are spared this emotional lashing. The loss of a life companion in any situation is devastating, but other diseases don't evoke the distress and fear that one might also die of the same thing.

AIDS seems to bring out the worst in people, not in PLWAs but in others who prefer not to have anything to do with them. *Prefer* is too mild a word. People denounce and ostracize, pillory and punish PLWAS, even small children. A hemophiliac boy who contracted AIDS from a blood transfusion made local and then national headlines not long ago when he was so reviled and threatened by his schoolmates that his family was forced to move to a more accepting community. What a wretched and bitter sorrow for the boy and his family to endure! This boy taught everyone a lesson with his courage and forgiveness. How many children have to die to make us more compassionate to PLWAs?

More devastating is the attitude of the families of PLWAs: some of them abandon their own flesh and blood. PLWAs are dying in agony, alone in rented rooms with inadequate care or attention because their families want nothing to do with them, not because of the disease as such, but because of the stigmatization the disease causes. AIDS is spreading more and more rapidly throughout society, among drug users, women, and children: infants born with the disease contracted from their mothers, or children, as noted, who have been given a transfusion of HIV-positive blood. (Blood is being tested now but the disease is still being discovered and diagnosed among people, particularly hemophiliacs who received blood before the screening was required.)

AIDS is a life-threatening disease. It leads to death by diseases that have invaded a body whose immune system has been wiped out. The options include any one of a number of horrible, agonizing deaths: a particularly virulent form of pneumonia, a new strain of cancer.

A "buddy" system has grown out of the AIDS epidemic, started because so many of the early PLWAs were deserted by their families. They needed someone to help them. As the illness progresses, the PLWA can no longer hold down a job. Income goes as expenses pile up for medication and treatment. A buddy is sometimes the PLWA's lover, sometimes not; most times a compassionate volunteer. He or she serves as much more than a buddy or companion to the PLWA. The services involve health care, feeding, and support, both emotional and financial. A person can't be a buddy for too long, for obvious reasons. After a buddy has buried two or three PLWAs, he or she may have reached burnout and have to withdraw to recover.

All these factors make for high emotional stress and soul-destroying anguish. The whole menu of the stages of grief is there *à la carte*. No one has to take his pick, though; he gets it all: shock, denial, anger, bargaining, depression, but very little acceptance — more like resignation, or tight-lipped horror. As does every crisis, AIDS brings out the best and worst in people.

I have already mentioned the worst: families, including parents, who turn their backs on their own. When the compassion does succeed in breaking down shame and prejudice, it has been the mother more frequently than the father who opens her arms and cares for her adult child. The denial and rejection by fathers of PLWAs can follow them like a painful dart to the grave. I have noted elsewhere some of society's cruelty to children who have contracted AIDS. Women, more at risk than previously considered, have been either almost entirely ignored in the huge draughts of denial sweeping over this whole, sad situation or else pilloried as outcasts. These are the worst aspects of AIDS.

The best thing that comes out of these tragic deaths is love — enormous, flowing oceans of love. The care and devotion of (some) families and (most) lovers bear moving witness to the humanity of the people involved, if there was ever any doubt. It seems some people still have to be convinced.

Paul Monette was a Hollywood writer living the good life with his long-time lover when AIDS shattered their dream. Monette's book *Borrowed Time*, which won the 1989 PEN West U.S.A. Literary Award for Best Nonfiction, is a powerfully moving account of the last nineteen months of his lover's life. "The story I want to tell," he writes, "is about heroism and sacrifice and love, but I will not be avoiding the anger."

If one needed to see the stages of grief blueprinted, one could look only to this book. Every phase is humanly, movingly documented — and beautifully expressed. "I have come to be more godless than anyone I know after all this meaningless suffering," Monette writes bitterly. But then he confesses, "I cannot say what pagan god it was, but I'd gotten in the habit, last thing at night, of praying: *Thank you for this*."

This may be grace in action, this ability, this need, to give thanks for whatever small blessings each day may bring. We find the skill of grace among those dying from whatever cause and also among the survivors: a persistent gratitude for whatever small, treasured favors life still bestows. But what of the people who opt for despair, that is, those who choose to end their lives? And what of those who aid and abet them? What grace then?

Edwin Schneidman, founder of the American Association for Suicidology, has coined the phrase *survivor/victim* for the loved ones, family, and friends of suicides — an estimated seven to ten people deeply affected by each of the thirty thousand to fifty thousand people who commit suicide each year in North America. Adolescent suicides, particularly, leave two distinct sets of survivor/victims: their families and their close contemporaries.

Those bereaved by suicide experience the stages of grief in megadoses: tidal waves of shock, particularly if the survivor/victim is the one to discover the body; soul-shattering denial and guilt in equal compounds; enough rage to burn down a forest. The emotions are even more devastating because they are accompanied by an insinuating sense of helplessness and a complete lack of control, all suffered in a ghastly, awesome, crippling, muffled silence. No one wants to talk about suicide and no one wants to listen. Small wonder that suicides often beget suicides: two (or more) in a family are not uncommon. According to the American Association of Suicidology, survivor/victims are more likely to kill themselves than are the rest of the population. Once suicide has happened, it becomes an option to others involved.

Suicide is the second killer (after accidents) of young people; what is not realized is that suicide is a far more common cause of death among the elderly than among the young. The suicide rate among widowers in the first year following bereavement is much higher than the general population, as it is for widows in their second year of bereavement. No bargain appears possible to a suicide; death looks like the only way out. Suicide survivor/victims, more than any other bereaved, need therapy to help them say their final farewell to and negotiate their peace with the departed before it's too late and they take matters into their own hands.

Sometimes others take our matters into their hands. More than any other kind of death, murder traumatizes society as well as the immediate survivors. We all feel threatened and unsafe after a murder in our midst. Equal parts shock and terror rock our safe foundations and make us waver in our trust not only in life, but in predictable behavior. More frightening to me is the fact that such deaths are not entirely unpredictable. Apart from the victims, both child and adult, of serial killers, usually chosen at random, the majority of murdered women are killed by someone known to them, that is, a lover or husband. We must acknowledge the fact that we live in a violent society and brace ourselves for grief, even while we seek peace.

I will deal with the deaths of infants in more detail, but I want to say a word here about abortion. Right-to-Lifers may not believe this, but women who opt for an abortion also go through some of the stages of grief and they pray over their decision:

> Creator take you, sky enfold you, stars remember you,
>   powers return you.
> Tomorrow we will die.
> — LINDA GRIFFITHS, "PRAYER BEFORE AN ABORTION,"
>   from THE DARLING FAMILY

In her book, *In a Different Voice*, Carol Gilligan reports on interviews with women who had chosen abortion; none of them made the choice lightly or without anguish. Stillbirths, miscarriages, agonizingly short lives snuffed out—all these early losses inflict their pain and must be recognized among all the kinds of death I am considering.

Such a disheartening panoply from which to choose our pain! In the end there isn't much to choose among them, that is, it's not our choice. One out of one dies of something.

IV

DEATH OF A HUMAN BEING

Diminished inexorably by others' deaths,
one wonders how much there is to let go,
until the final farewell.

9. Loss of a Parent

Their death isn't the sorrow I thought it
would be, the passion and pain,
More the bewilderment of a child left out in the rain.
— ELIZABETH SMART

To lose one parent . . . may be regarded as a misfortune;
to lose both looks like carelessness.
— OSCAR WILDE

THE LOSS OF A PARENT FINALLY MAKES ONE BELIEVE IN ONE'S own mortality. The survivors — that is, the children of the departed mother or father — become the grownups and are supposed to inherit the wisdom and the maturity and the god-like control sufficient to look after the succeeding generations. Strange, for such heady power to arrive with such a reminder of the weakness of us all, that is, with the death of a parent, proof positive that no one lives forever, not even our omnipotent forbears.

"Each man's death diminishes me," wrote John Donne, but especially, perhaps, the death of a parent. This is a blood relative we're talking about, one's kin, one's flesh and blood. Diminishment becomes very personal and affects not only the psyche, but one's sense of self-preservation. After all, the nature of the death may indicate a genetic legacy, some foreboding of one's own death. I know several men who regard the anniversary of their father's death-date and the cause of death with more than casual apprehension. They seem to consider the date a milestone to pass, and guard against whatever fatal disease it was as their only nemesis. (My father always expected to die from a heart attack, like his father.)

There are other emotional burdens connected with the death of a parent. When one parent dies, then the remaining one (usually the mother) requires more help, both financial and physical, and some sort of social life as well. The caregiver (usually the daughter) steps into the breach, has already done so in the case of a long, devastating illness. Role-reversals cause anxiety as well as grief. An adult child thus suffers before as well as after the fact of the parent's death.

At whatever age the death of a parent strikes, it's too soon and very frightening. To a young child the death of a young parent is incomprehensible and overwhelming. Sorrow follows its usual basic pattern: shock, denial, anger — and maybe acceptance, but it keeps on having to be renegotiated as the child grows older. In a child, the first symptoms of shock may very well be ignored because the adult household — that is, the surviving parent, grandparents, siblings, and so on — is caught up with the immediate logistics of death. No one pays too much attention to the lack of appetite or the loss of sleep the child suffers because everyone is in an abnormal state and on an irregular routine. Nothing is normal; anything is appropriate, or at least not surprising. A child's frantic screams or unnatural silence can both indicate intense grief, but no one seems to pay any attention or to mind.

Writer William Maxwell, in his semi-autobiographical novel *So Long, See You Tomorrow*, deals summarily with his mother's death from double pneumonia, two days after the birth of the author's younger brother. "After that," he says, "there were no more disasters. The worst that could happen had happened, *and the shine went out of everything*" (emphasis mine). No one in the household seemed to know what to do about it. He says that it all seemed like a mistake.

Denial in young children, even up to the age of eight, is almost automatic. They have played "Bang-you're-dead" games and the dead guys always get up, don't they? So why not now? Daddy or Mommy couldn't be dead. He or she is coming back — soon. Young children often ask for the return of the missing parent for a birthday or Christmas present, yet somehow they know that there are no longer any guarantees. Fairy-tale happy endings and wishes do not come true. Nothing is sure. Safety and security are gone, never again to be assumed as a given or a right. The fear then extends to the thought of other people and things disappearing without warning.

Denial goes hand over fist with fear, plus something like guilt. If the child has recently expressed anger at the parent ("I hate you! I wish you were dead!") for any reason, then self-accusation and blame and guilt surround the death ("I caused it. It's my fault"). Then there is the fear that, if this unforeseen, impossible event took place, there is no safety in the world. Terror mounts, followed by tears and accusations and anger.

I don't think I handled their father's death very well for my children. Years later, John told me he had something like 130 detentions in the months following his loss, and Kate told me she spent six months screaming at her boyfriend. Liz was off to her first year in university — heavy stress for her — and Matt missed his Dad worse than anyone. I was scarcely aware of anything but fear, trying to figure out how to make a living for us all. It's not that I didn't care; I just didn't know what to do.

I met a widower whose wife had committed suicide, and his children were worse off than mine: the older one, a girl, quit school, while the younger boy failed for a couple of years until he was put in a private school. Another widower whose wife died of cancer had trouble keeping his son out of juvenile court for several years, and finally went the route of tough love to try to pull the boy on course. It's not an easy time for anyone.

I did know instinctively that grief should never be bottled up. Too often young (and not-so-young) children are told not to cry, that crying will hurt the surviving parent, that tears won't do any good, that they have to be brave little soldiers or good little helpers and very grown-up now that this sad thing has happened. To send grief thus underground is to plant a time bomb that will explode later in a much more damaging way. As with everyone else, grief in a child must be acknowledged, allowed expression, and respected.

More frequently than a parent, a grandparent is the first loved adult human being to leave a child's life. It depends on the family, of course, but this relationship can be very close, and the loss of it very painful. Again, the child's loss can be overlooked and minimized, because one of the parents is suffering the death of a parent. The child may be shuffled out of the way (as I was) and not even told the news until later.

Rabbi Earl Grollman was asked when a child was old enough to attend a funeral. Not knowing the answer, he said, he made up a number: "Eight." But I read in the book *Widower* of a very young widower who held a family wake with an open coffin. His three-year-old son and eighteen-month-old daughter and his children's cousins kept running up to the coffin to kiss the body, laughing and running away. The father didn't figure out what they had been doing until several years later when he was rereading a fairy tale to his son and the boy said, "Oh, look, there's my Mommy," pointing to the picture of Sleeping Beauty. Children take in only as much as they understand, no more. Adults, too.

What children understand best is the continuing absence of their parent, and the absence of normality. Father's Day without Father, Mother's Day without Mother, first day of school without one of the parents, any time of day with someone important missing. Intense grieving may recur again and again with each fresh reminder of the loss.

A parable: "Mommy," said a little boy of my acquaintance when George VI died (the boy was little then), "why is all the sad music on the radio?" "Because," said his mother, "the King has died and gone to Heaven, a wonderful, happy place where departed souls go." "That's nice, Mommy." Long pause. "Why is all the sad music on the radio?"

What we say to our children about God and Heaven and the afterlife will have an effect on them too. Kindly people click their tongues and say it — whatever tragedy or disaster "it" was — was "God's will," thereby running the risk of making the child permanently angry at God. Or they say, "God took your Mommy/Daddy," causing the same resentment, anger, and fear.

Especially fear. What's to stop God from taking the child as well? Death doesn't really enter into people's conscious thoughts until it forcibly attracts their attention. A child who has lost a parent understandably loses trust in life. Life is not as certain as it seemed, and never will be again. This uncertainty, this anxiety easily transfers to the surviving parent. Young children will cling unashamedly, whereas older ones will be full of practical worries and become very solicitous about the safe driving and good health habits (no smoking!) on the part of the remaining parent.

Any expression — be it concern, anger, blame, fear, whatever — must be expected and not shamed into silence. Ultimatums like "I never want to hear you speak like that again!" or panaceas like "Hush now, you'll get over it" or "Don't worry, everything's going to be fine" will not do. Reassurances, however, will help, accompanied by as much information as the child can bear. Any new living or care arrangements should be spelled out and prepared for, not just sprung on the child. Just as grieving adults do, grieving children think of seeming irrelevancies in the midst of grief:

- "Who will make chocolate pudding for me now?"
- "Can I still go to camp?"
- "Will I still get an allowance?"
- "Who's going to help me with my math?"

Too trivial to be genuine concern, too selfish to be real grief? Not so. The self is always involved in death. Any loss involves adjustment to the inevitable change. Therefore, any question regarding the change is totally legitimate, and should never be brushed aside.

What bereaved children need, what we all need, is communication: talk and more talk, and, of course, someone on the other end to listen.

My twelve-year-old son, Matt, was sitting on a chair near his father when Bill dropped his glass and pitched forward, with his head on the coffee table. Matt kept talking about the glass that fell. "What happened to the glass?" he kept asking for about a week. Matt is brain-damaged, and I used to play teaching games with him. The game we were playing at that time was like Fish: matching pairs, but these pairs were homonyms, words that sound alike, but are spelled differently and mean different things. Once discovered, a pair is claimed by using each of the words correctly in a sentence — good teaching therapy. For weeks, Matt managed to make every sentence he uttered invoke his father's death; he talked about graves and funerals, die, dead, death, tombstones, and coffins, and that fallen glass. That was good recovery therapy too.

Matt was the child who showed me how worried he was about me. I had driven us up for a weekend at the lake with friends and Matt was to stay on, but, when the time came for me to drive home alone, he wouldn't let me go without him. He had to watch over me and make sure I didn't die on him, too.

Five years after Bill's death, three years after we had moved to Toronto, I took Matt back to Stratford with me for a few days. We went to the theater, we visited friends; some former neighbors had a party for Matt. As we drove out of town, Matt burst into tears, really heavy sobs, and said he wished his Dad hadn't died. I realized he thought that, if his father hadn't died, nothing would have changed. That's when I tried to explain to him about loss and change and time like a river. Even if

Dad were alive, I said, even if he hadn't died, life would not be the same. Other neighbors would have moved away; Matt's three older siblings would have left home, no matter what; I would have spent more time writing as all of them became more independent, and in all probability, we ourselves would not have stayed in Stratford. You can't go back, Matthew. No one can. Even if that particular something hadn't happened, something else would have.

Older children, too, may feel that the bottom has dropped out of life when a parent dies. It has. Teenagers are vulnerable in other ways than some I have already mentioned. For one thing, they don't want to be singled out. They don't want to be seen as strange or different, perhaps threatening to their peers. They have enough trouble coping with their emotions without having to deal with terminal illness in a parent and the subsequent death, or for that matter with a sudden death, death of any kind (hardest of all is suicide, seen as rejection and blame). After the fact, they may feel trapped by the man-of-the-house-little-helper lines but also by their own sense of responsibility: "How can *I* ever leave when I am needed?" Or else they feel rejected and left out, as when a new person enters the bereaved parent's life, thereby, so the thinking goes, burying for good and forever the memory of the deceased one. As with anyone, fear for the self is uppermost in a teenager's mind, and survival is the goal.

The bereaved parent, engrossed, tends to forget that the children are undergoing similar grief symptoms. Children should be given credit for deep feelings and granted permission, even encouraged, to express them. The surviving parent and children are the only ones who have suffered this most cutting loss. If they can share their pain, they will help each other to survive.

An older child — the adult offspring — sustains, as I suggested, a different kind of loss on the death of an aged parent, or parents. Elder of the tribe now, the senior citizen, but feeling as helpless and incompetent as on the first day of school, this bereaved adult child loses not only the parent but also possibly one of the few people who granted unconditional love and approval. I say *possibly*, because not all parents warmly approve of their grown children.

I suffered one of the darker nights of my soul in the hours between the doctor's nocturnal announcement to me of my mother's imminent death and my last trip to the hospital in the morning.

I had been my father's daughter; my brother Jack was his mother's son. It wasn't until after my husband's sudden death that Mother's and my relationship began to improve. Suddenly she pitied me. Slowly I sympathized with her. However, our visits were never unalloyed pleasure. We loved each other but we couldn't live with each other for longer than three days.

Then my mother got old. She'd had a couple of small implosions — blackouts or mini-strokes — that had rendered her unconscious or amnesiac for anywhere from a few minutes up to half an hour. She didn't tell me; a cousin of mine reported this news. Mother had put herself on the waiting list of a retirement home because her fierce independence had suddenly been compromised by fear.

The apartment down the hall from me had just come up for sale, a studio. I phoned my mother and proposed moving her east to live in that studio, close to me, where I could keep an eye on her and be there when she needed me. She accepted with alacrity. Maybe it was a bad decision. Maybe she realized she had made a terrible mistake in moving away from her last home in her home town. There was no going back, however. Instead, she died.

Only five months after my mother had moved in as my neighbor, an embolism in her small intestine took a week to kill her. The young doctor I had found to make house calls hadn't spotted it when he came to discover the reason for her increasing malaise; she was so riddled with arthritis it was difficult to localize any one source of her escalating pain. Instead, he asked me if she was angry at me for any reason. He asked, he said, because he smelled the sweet fragrance of starvation on her breath, and wanted to know if she was on a hunger strike. I had been away on an assignment and had noticed her reluctance to have me leave. (I think now it was fear, not resentment, on Mother's part.) The doctor's words made me feel trapped. I thought I was being emotionally blackmailed and I did not respond gracefully.

It never even crossed my mind that she was dying. She was eighty-two years old but I thought she was immortal. Her older sister was still going strong at age ninety-one. I thought I would be caring for my mother for at least ten more years. So when she called me later that evening to say she was in pain, I went quickly but with no deeper concern than I had felt all week. It wasn't until a couple of hours later, when I realized that I could not spend the night with her in a room with only one bed and that she was unable to spend the night at my place because she wasn't strong enough to walk down the hall, that I finally faced my own helplessness. I called an ambulance because I had run out of things I could do for her. It remains to my everlasting shame and regret that, when she needed her forehead sponged, I handed her a dampened facecloth instead of doing it for her. I have been wiping foreheads ever since in Mother's name and to her memory, though I cannot sponge away my guilt. The next morning, in expiation, I washed all my mother's woollens in preparation for spring.

The surgeon optimistically diagnosed the trouble as a twisted intestine, not a bad guess about a patient who was incoherent with pain. I gave permission for immediate surgery but it was too late. The embolism was discovered; the small intestine had already become gangrenous; nothing could be done. Mother was brought back to her hospital bed to die, within ten or twelve hours, the doctor warned me at 1:00 a.m. the night after my Facecloth Denial. I made some essential phone calls and tried to come to peace within myself before I went to say goodbye to my mother.

She was in a coma but I am convinced that the spirit remains sentient and that some deep consciousness keeps working even in those who are unconscious. So I talked to my mother. I laid my hands on her — the hands I had denied her twenty-four hours earlier — and stroked her forehead and face and read her two psalms. First, 121: "I will lift up mine eyes unto the hills, from whence cometh my help." And then 23: "The Lord is my shepherd; I shall not want." I prayed aloud over my mother (talking to God, to her, and to myself) and assured her that it was all right to leave.

"It's over," I said. "You've done a good job. You're free to join Daddy. Don't try to wait for Jack to come. You don't have to wait any longer. Goodbye, Mom." At last, I made my peace with my mother.

Strange pieces of madness remain stuck in one's mind. I came back later the same day with my older daughter to find that my mother had just died; a nurse had tried to phone me even as I was en route to the hospital. I saw the bulky white plastic bodybag on the bed, tagged and ready to be picked up by the undertaker for cremation, as I had arranged in sad anticipation. Almost a year later, after Christmas, when my kids were helping me take down the tree, the bulky orange bag they thrust it in suddenly reminded me of my mother in her bag and I was shaking all over with some kind of terror or anguish — pain, anyway. We all get stuck with images like that, little booby-traps in our minds that catch us when we aren't looking.

As to the cremation, there was a crematorium, as it turned out, in my end of the city, just ten minutes' walk from my apartment, a fact I had paid no attention to until I needed to know it. I arranged to pick up the ashes there, planning to fly to Winnipeg later that day for their interment with my father. I remember getting up that morning, singing a paraphrase of an old song: "This is the day they give ashes away, with half a pound of tea," as I dressed and trotted off to my friendly neighborhood crematorium.

The trouble with me is I have no imagination. I had *no idea*, no preconceived notion, never gave it a thought, as to how I would feel when I was handed the cardboard box holding my mother's ashes. I was numb at first as I tucked her under my arm and stumbled out of the building, then blinded with the tears streaming down my face, scarcely noticing the lights on the street I had to cross to reach home. It happened that a cassette was waiting in my mail, the first taping of the music Quenten Doolittle had written to my lyrics for a musical adaptation of *The Second Shepherds' Play*. I played it and heard the music to these words:

> *Peace, peace,*
> *So the angels sing.*
> *Bow down before*
> *Your heavenly king.*

And I was comforted. The theology may not suit everyone, but faith in something is implicit in the acknowledgment of death, if only faith in life. No matter what level of spiritual sophistication — or simplicity — a person has reached, life claims attention and death demands awe. Grief is the tribute paid by everyone who has loved life or self. Grief is the blessing as well as the wound.

My mother and I may have had our differences but when she died I lost the last person who was totally on my side. She might not have understood me, she might have found a lot to criticize, but I was her daughter, right or wrong. Though we might have disagreed in private, she would defend me to others with her life and breath. Now I have no one and I'm the top of the totem.

A long terminal illness presents grief in a different context when a parent is dying. The certain (or denied) knowledge of impending death requires grief work on the part of the one dying but it also imposes anticipatory grief on the survivors, both adult and child. Le Anne Schreiber, in her book *Midstream*, describes her mother's terminal illness. Her father was the primary caregiver and Schreiber came (for weeks and months at a time) when she could. She notes the difference in reactions between mate and adult child of the dying one: "The discrepancy between Dad's and my response to crucial moments is hard to take. I don't care if he sees what I see; I'm glad he doesn't see any more trauma than he does. But after such moments I need time and privacy to heal my wounds, and he is often full of a garrulous optimism that makes my head feel it is being squeezed with a barbed-wire tourniquet."

Children can feel very left out when the family focuses on a dying parent. Household routines are totally upset, comforting hugs and reassurances are often minimal, rushed, brushed aside. Not only is the sick parent unavailable, but the healthy one is too busy to pay attention. Hospitals generally do not allow children under a certain age to visit, and the child often has to stay in the waiting room for hours. In any case, parents fear that the sight of the ill one, with all the tubes and bottles and perhaps with a drastic change in appearance, may terrorize the child. If there has been no denial, and death is acknowledged as a certainty, then fear of the future without that parent compounds the present pain. The usual symptoms of shock, denial, and anger pile up with little or no reconciliation possible.

I know of one dying father who thought of a way to reassure his child that he still cared. He arranged for his brother to take the little girl out of the waiting room to see a surprise from her Dad. The surprise was in the family car — a trunkload of toys and dolls and games — and, best of all, the girl's father, gaunt but smiling, with his head out the window of his hospital room, and waving down at her.

Children's help can be enlisted so that they feel part of the team. If some small errands are assigned to them within their capacity to perform, and some confidences shared, some advice requested — again within their capacity to receive and judge — then they will not feel so left out. Care and time should also be taken to explain to them the arrangements being made for their future when the parent has died. A child needs reassurance that the bottom of the world isn't going to drop away; it is, but a little reassurance helps.

Adult children who bear the burden of physical care of an aging and terminally ill parent, as well as the incipient grief, have the same reactions as young children, with the additional threat of possible burnout. They may also be attempting to care for the other, well parent, not only easing the strain of physical care of the dying one but also trying to tend to the emotional onslaught on the other one. Further, the two adults, parent and child, may not see eye to eye. One may still be in the denial stage while the other has progressed, if you can call it that, to anger or depression. There is a lot of denial flying around in families at the best of times; illness tends to increase it — enough negative power to cause an area-wide blackout.

No matter whether the person is dying or saying goodbye to a person who is dying, listening and paying attention are vital. Sometimes, the soon-to-be-bereaved needs this attention even more than the one who is leaving. In there, in the eye of the storm, the dying one is coping breath by breath, adjusting to the shutdown of the temple. Out here, torn between the living world we're supposed to be functioning in and this inner world of peace and terror mingled, we vacillate. We waver between seeing the dying parent (or anyone of whose dying we have an intimate knowledge) as a person greater than the sum of the disease, infection, and physical disintegration we witness daily, or as a spirit that will leave us when it leaves its body. We care for the body while it endures, but we also need to minister to that spirit and prepare both of us for silence. This is all part of the grieving.

It goes on. So does our life, after a parent's death, a little more vulnerable.

10. Loss of a Child

To lose a spouse is like losing a limb; to lose a child is like losing a lung.
— BEREAVED FAMILIES OF ONTARIO BROCHURE

TIME WAS, NOT SO LONG AGO, THAT THE DEATH OF A CHILD was a common occurrence. Mary Vial Holyoke was a Boston woman who gave birth twelve times; three of her children survived to adulthood. One little boy, Edward Augustus, was born April 8, 1782. Here is Mary Holyoke's diary entry for September 1 of that year: "My Dear Child Died 9 a.m., which makes the 8th Child." What a wealth of pain is implicit in that sad statistic!

The expectation of death, the awareness of the fragility of life, theoretically prevented too great an investment of hope and affection until a strong child gave some assurance of continuing existence and warranting some investment of affection. Children in an earlier age were not immediately named, or if they were, not distinctively (John I, II, III, etc.) because they were, not expendable or disposable, but surely — transitory. Even so, cries come echoing down the centuries, hinting at the agony caused by the death of a child.

Here is Queen Elizabeth in *Richard III* (IV, iv, 9–14) lamenting the death of the young princes:

Ah, my poor princes! ah, my tender babes! . . .
My unblown flowers, new-appearing sweets!

If yet your gentle souls fly in the air
And be not fix'd in doom perpetual,
Hover about me with your airy wings,
And hear your mother's lamentation!

And here is Lady Capulet in *Romeo and Juliet* (IV, v, 47–49) upon learning of Juliet's (seeming) death:

But one, poor one, one poor and loving child,
But one thing to rejoice and solace in,
And cruel death hath catch'd it from my sight!

And Juliet's father (IV, v, 63–64):

Alack, my child is dead;
And with my child my joys are buried.

In literature, characters are given the insights and observations of their creator. Real people, even writers, dealing with their own lives, are often less articulate. However, they leave quiet hints of searing pain. I offer as an example a small sampling from the diary of Mary Shelley, wife of the poet, and the creator of *Frankenstein*. Her life wasn't easy: three of her four children died, and she had one miscarriage. She was only twenty-four years old when her husband drowned.

On March 6, 1815, Shelley reported the death of her infant son in a few words: "Find my baby dead. . . . Talk. A miserable day. . . ." On March 7, her diary entry reads: "Shelley and Clara go after breakfast to town. . . . Not in good spirits. . . . A fuss. To bed at 3."

Today with antisepsis, incubators, antibiotics, infant blood replacement, heart transplants, and all the magic medicine that can pull live rabbits out of hats, that is, live babies out of wombs, parents have grown to expect the safe delivery of a healthy baby. (It isn't always perfect, and I'll deal with damaged children in a later chapter.) When the miraculous has become commonplace, if something does go wrong, the disappointment and grief are bitterly magnified. "We expected a crib not a coffin," say bereaved parents, "and baby cards not sympathy cards."

Thirty years ago, the baby boy of a woman I know died at four days. He stopped breathing while still in the hospital. The baby was bundled into a grave, and the bereaved mother was sent home with a prescription for hefty doses of Valium, the 1960s' solution to women's little problems. She still mourns that child.

They're like closet skeletons, these ghosts of children past. Some of their stories were told to me by friends and acquaintances who wanted to share a grief with me when my husband died: a four-year-old girl drowned in a water-filled post-hole when a fence was being built to keep her safe in her back yard; another little girl died of leukemia; a little boy died at two weeks of meningitis, another one of cancer; a three-week-old baby girl died of SIDS (Sudden Infant Death Syndrome). It's no surprise that these deaths occur; no family or human being lives without loss. The revelation was that my sad statistic gave these people an opportunity, an excuse, to tell me of their loss. No one ever wanted to hear. Spirits of the dead keep whispering to us in our sorrow but no one wants to listen.

That is why a support system is being developed to help people deal with the loss of an infant. The professionals have not been much help. In most of the stories I have heard or read, brusque doctors do not emerge as sensitive champions of bereaved parents. Their timing and delivery of bad news are almost uniformly and notoriously callous and their comments are less than helpful:

- "Don't blame yourself."
- "Don't worry. It's all for the best."
- "Good fruit doesn't fall."
- "You'll have another baby before you know it."
- "Why not try again?"

Not to be too hard on doctors. They see too much. They can't afford to be too vulnerable for fear they will be unable to continue. Like most people, they have a fear of failure. A dead baby is a definite failure. That's why the obstetrician says to the mother, "Don't blame yourself," thereby shifting the blame to her and exonerating himself.

Well-meaning friends, with less justification, aren't much better:

- "It's a good thing it died before you got too attached to it."
- "Cheer up, there's always a next time."
- "It's a good thing you already have a child/children."
- "Think of the work you've saved."

These are not invented comments; real people made them. Few people remember to include the bereaved new father in their clumsy condolences. All the concern and questions are directed at the mother. The father answers the phone and a solicitous voice asks how his wife is, with not a word for him. Granted, the baby was a greater physical reality to the mother during the pregnancy, but the father has also suffered a loss and should be included in the comfort and support. Here are some lines from a poem by a father mourning his newborn's death:

> Your mother cried without shame
> twice wounded and still bloody
> Shattered dreams drive sharp splinters deep
> I do believe in miracles
> but used them up years ago
> No tears for me, the cursed strong shoulder, no tears
>
> Suburban sanctuary
> attainable aspirations
> I offered you bonds   guaranteed
> income   certificates in escrow
> inscribed with a name never
> once uttered aloud
> But you traded me for flowers.
> — STEVE STANTON, "CERTIFICATE IN ESCROW"

Men are distressed, perhaps for the very fact that they had no physical relationship with the growing embryo. By miscarriage, stillbirth, or death within days, they lose a phantom. "It's very hard," said one bereaved father, "to say goodbye before you've even had a chance to say hello." Men are woefully hindered by society's injunction not to cry. I saw a father on television, being interviewed with his wife, after they had given up their newborn infant's heart that another baby might live. Their child had been born without a brain and would not have lived more than a few days. The father described taking his baby in his arms "and walking over to the hospital window to show. . . ." He had to stop; if he had said any more he would have broken down. His wife took over: " . . . the light and the color outside," she finished his sentence for him. "It was important," she said. He pinched his lips together and nodded.

What is considered important now is that the tiny dead babe be properly mourned: named, held, acknowledged, grieved. People question how soon the young can be introduced to death. I was told of a young family, a six-year-old girl and a four-year-old boy whose father brought them to the hospital to see their mother and dead sibling.

"Is my brother dead?" asked the six-year-old.

"When's she going to get up?" asked the four-year-old.

"This isn't like Bang-you're-dead," said the father. "This dead is forever."

Forever, of course, is the rest of the survivors' lives. So for the sake of forever, this present time of letting go mustn't be rushed. The family needs time.

A perinatal bereavement team at Women's College Hospital in Toronto, working with bereaved new parents since 1982, has prepared a kit to help parents. The kit comprises several booklets including one entitled *Healing a Father's Grief*, and a list of books families could read to their other children to help them understand the loss. The bereavement team has drawn up a Bill of Rights for parents and babies to enable families to absorb their loss. The "Rights of Parents" begins with the simple one of being given the opportunity to see, hold, and touch their baby at any time before and after death.

This was a startling and new idea when first introduced; the infant corpse used to be rushed away, and the new mother never saw or touched her child. Another revolutionary idea, which had to be carried out initially without consent from the hospital authorities was to give the parents the opportunity to photograph their baby; corollary to that is the opportunity to be given as many mementoes as possible: the hospital bracelet, the birth and death certificate (legally necessary), the cards received, and so on. The opportunity to name the child enables parents to bond to it and put a label on their loss, rather than on some nameless creature. Of course, parents should be permitted to observe any religious or cultural practices and to plan burial or cremation according to their traditions and needs. They should be fully informed, and they should be allowed to request an autopsy. The parents should be permitted to be with each other during the hospital stay and they are entitled to be cared for by an empathetic staff.

As for the "Rights of the Baby," he or she should be acknowledged as a *person* who was born and died, and to be named, if that is the parents' wish. The dying or dead infant should be seen and touched and held by the family, for this way lies reality. The parents, say the team, have the right to say goodbye to their little hope.

Grandparents, too, should not be forgotten. The parents of newly bereaved parents have a double-edged pain: the disappointment, certainly, at the loss of a grandchild, but also the helplessness at being unable to wipe away the pain of their adult child. They can't make it better. If a grandmother has suffered a similar loss in her childbearing years, she may be shocked, even horrified at the different attitudes and treatment today. She may be shocked, anyway. A lot of people are. They recoil, thinking it morbid to hold a dying or dead infant, especially an abnormal one. The parents, however, feel relief, not horror. The mother, after nine months of pregnancy, finds it difficult to absorb the loss, to believe it really has happened. The hallucinations common to the bereaved may even convince her the babe is still in her womb, kicking. For the father, who has not experienced prenatal bonding, as the mother has, it may be even more important that he sees and touches and holds the child he has lost.

Loss, as I have said, continues. Loss is permanent. Parents who lose a child at birth keep on grieving for what might have been, remembering the birth and death dates (sometimes the same date) as the years pass, and making a mental emotional note of milestones that might have been, a calendar of non-events, like the first day of school, or graduation day, and so on, including the hopes, dreams, and fantasies of other siblings. One of my daughters, who had a miscarriage between the births of her two children, commented just recently how much closer a playmate the lost baby would have been to her older child. Life may end but death doesn't; it keeps on happening, and we keep on having to come to terms with it.

These days relatively few people know what it's like to lose a baby — or any child. "When you lose a mate, you lose the past; when you lose a child, you lose the future," says Bereaved Families of Ontario. One has to be careful of the future. Any parent raising children develops a vivid imagination in the attempt to anticipate and prevent fatal accidents. (I am obviously not talking about parents who inflict grievous bodily damage, even to the point of death, on their children. That is another subject entirely.) No parent, however vigilant, can completely accident-proof a child's life, and there is no way, in spite of all the vaccines and inoculations available now, of circumventing a terminal illness.

Elisabeth Kübler-Ross, in my opinion, has been most successful and comforting in her hospice programs for dying children. Death and youth in our present context seem to be incompatible, a contradiction in terms, more than they were in centuries past. So it is now that we cling to the thought of long life for our children, expecting that they will outlive us — of course they will!

The denial and anger Kübler-Ross describes in the stages of dying are rampant during a child's terminal illness and can even damage the relationship between parent and child, and — even more commonly — between parents and their other, healthy children. If the terminal illness is a lengthy one, the care (and its expense) of the dying child becomes a career in itself, unbalancing the entire family and often causing strange, long-term side effects that reach far into the grieving that continues after the death.

Following the death of a child after a long illness, parents and siblings will discover that they have lost parts of themselves and each other. The loss is more than physical and personal; it involves their dreams of recovery, fantasies of renewal, hopes for the future, all the emotional investment one places in a child and tomorrow. The hopeless terminal illness of a child has to be one of the most harrowing painful experiences parents can go through. They want to do everything they can to seek a cure, to eliminate pain, to wipe away fear, to the point of neglecting each other, ignoring the grandparents, and not responding to the needs of their other children, if any. A sick child can easily dominate a household, to no one's ultimate good. And yet, although every wish may be honored as a command, all too frequently true communication breaks down. The child and the parents both may be all too aware of the impending death, and yet both are tongue-tied, afraid of calling a spade a spade and of admitting the imminent need to dig a grave with it.

With all the attention focused on the parents' pain when a child dies, the surviving child or children are likely to be lost in the slow, reluctant shuffle to the grave. If the dead sibling suffered a long-term illness, the ones at home have already experienced some envy and fear. They get the impression that the wrong one is dying, that it should be one the parents don't care as much about losing. They have already realized that their lives and activities are not as important to their parents — that, if they died, they wouldn't even be missed.

In the case of a sudden death, the surviving siblings often feel guilty. If they'd had a fight recently (and who hasn't had?), then they blame themselves for their rancor. If they were involved in the accident, whether observing and helpless or innocent participants, then they feel more guilt. They think they should have done something, or that it was their fault — even when it wasn't.

They are also really frightened, for the first time in their lives. If it's so easy to die, or if it's so hard, if it hurts so much, but is so impossible to prevent, then what or who can stop death happening to anyone? Suddenly they fear their own mortality. Every child at some time fantasizes the events of death — look at Tom Sawyer, who got to see his own wake. Mark Twain knew it was every child's fantasy. We all wonder if we'll be missed when we're gone. Children who see how much their sibling is missed can't help but wonder about their own demise.

We all have milestones and stop signs in our psyches. We see them in others: widows who program themselves to last until the children are grown and on their own before they let go and die; men who dread and often do not pass their own father's death date without a clutch of fear if not an actual stroke or heart attack. So a younger child will dread coming up to the age of the sibling and the death date. What if there is a stop sign waiting there?

Sometimes parents (fathers especially, it has been my observation) will wipe out anything to do with the dead child — all mementoes, pictures, reminders — and they forbid mention of the child's name, as if they hope that, by erasing memory, they can eliminate pain as well. Not only is this unhealthy for the parent, but such rejection can damage surviving children. They go through the rest of life believing that no one cares about them, that they will never be mourned when they die or be remembered longer than a ripple in a pond. Apparently, low self-esteem is common among children surviving the loss of a sibling. That, combined with the idealization of the one who dies, results in a slow, hidden, complicated, unresolved grief process.

There is a casting-off time, when the terminally ill person, child or adult, reaches the final stage of acceptance and turns away from life. Pain eases as the brain apparently releases massive doses of endorphins. If parents, siblings, and the dying child can only communicate then, an honest farewell will help to smooth the first rough stages of the grieving process after the fact.

The surprising sad bonus of this devastating farewell is that the survivors, that is, the parents, go through the first stages of grief with incredible speed. Martha Pearse Elliott, writing in Kübler-Ross's book *Living with Death and Dying*, comments on the "blessed relief" with which every parent finally greets the child's death. "There was an almost universal feeling of unshackling, of freedom to live without fear and pain again, but for themselves and for their dead children." Kübler-Ross's work and writing are all designed to facilitate this kind of leave-taking. We're on our way back to the "beautiful death."

But not everyone can die a good death. Children fall off balconies and out of trees and into water and under the wheels of cars. They burn themselves and cut themselves, and older ones do themselves grievous bodily harm on purpose or by an addiction that creeps up on them. Sudden death prevents both the child and the parents and family from preparing for separation and loss. The shock must be dealt with first, along with great chunks of denial, before any kind of reconciliation can be attempted. Anger, of course — a huge, overwhelming, seething wave of anger — is directed at the child; at the self for being unable to prevent the death; at the medical profession, or whatever convenient authority is handiest to blame, including God; at society; and at Fate, whatever that is.

Bereaved parents feel they have failed in their primary role as parents, that of protecting their child. As with any traumatic event, they have lost parts of self, but in the case of a child's death, they have lost the best part, the re-created self, the self that belonged, untarnished, to the future. They have lost a love that cannot be replaced, entirely different from the love of the life-companion. Above all, they have lost a piece of their immortality. No matter what anyone believes about a specific afterlife these days, most people will agree that a child represents continuing life, life after death — one's own death. The child is the link with life after one's own death. Now that, too, is gone, dead.

Again, showing how times and expectations have changed, we think today that a child's death is against nature. (It wasn't always so.) As the adult population increases, and people's average age rises, with all the improvements in nutrition and health care, odds are that the phenomenon — what is now considered a phenomenon — will increase as well, that more adult, aging parents will live to see the death of their grown, adult children. Then another loss becomes apparent: the seniors may well have lost the person who will look after them in their old age. This threat presents a fear that matches sorrow in its power to rivet the soul. We'll deal with age-grieving later, but this is one of its pressure points — the apprehension that we will outlive our caregivers.

I am pleased to report that the story is a myth, not borne out by statistics, that more marriages fall apart after the death of a child. There are certainly real strains on the relationship and on the family as a whole. In fact, connections change within the family unit in order for the remaining members to adjust to the empty space at the table and in the group. Often a family will find that a move will help all the members adjust to each other better. Various members feel neglected, unwanted, blamed, or ignored for a time and they respond with anger, fear, guilt, and defensive or offensive behavior. Grief must be permitted to all members of the family, and the need for grief must be acknowledged. Unresolved grief and unanswered questions that go underground now can cause horrendous repercussions later in life.

I know a family whose two small sons were having a pillow fight before bedtime, giggling and shouting and having a merry time, jumping from bed to bed and swatting each other with a bag full of feathers. The five-year-old dodged a wild swing from his four-year-old brother and laughed as the younger boy slipped and fell across the end of the bed, face forward, landing on his throat on the footboard. The laughter died when his brother didn't move. The esophagus had ruptured. The child was rushed to hospital but he was dead on arrival.

There were four other children; the family had a strong faith; they rallied round; they seemed to have absorbed their loss. Twenty years later, the father has discovered that his son considers himself to be a murderer. He still holds himself responsible for and guilty of the death of his brother. He thinks he bears the mark of Cain.

Twenty-one years ago, friends of friends of ours lost their five-year-old daughter in a car accident. She was run over on the street in front of their house. I saw the father recently, by chance, and he told me he couldn't bear to drive past that X-marks-the-spot and that was the reason he moved his wife and son to another city, another country. Ironically, their second daughter was born on the death date of the first one. (This happens, too, in families, these strange, fatally compelling ironies of date and time: a sibling is often born exactly on another's birth date, one or two years apart; my father died on his birthday.) Now the girl is twenty and acting out the unresolved grief of her parents, inaccessible as only a twenty-year-old can be, rebellious but needy — of she doesn't know what.

If society can't handle a person's mourning the death of a spouse, it has even more difficulty with parents' mourning a miscarriage or the death of a child. No wonder I was surprised to be told of a death in families I never suspected of hiding a secret sorrow. I discovered friends who had lost children I had never known about; no one ever allowed them to speak of it. Bereaved parents are hurt by society at every twist. It's almost as if they were being punished for their memories. In Act IV of Ibsen's *Brand*, Agnes, a bereaved mother, treasures her dead child's clothes:

> Here's the veil, the cloak my child
> Wore when at the font he smiled. —
> In this bundle is the dress —
> Blessings on his prettiness!
> Oh, my little lad looked sweet
> There upon the high church-seat!
> Here's the scarf, the coat, his wear
> The first time he took the air . . .
> Much too big he found them all,
> But they soon grew much too small . . .
> Mittens, bless the little lad!
> Stockings, — what a leg he had!
> New silk hood, to keep him warm
> In the very coldest storm:
> That's unworn, as good as new . . .
> Here his travelling clothes are, too:
> Wrapt in these, with cloak and rug,
> He should travel warm and snug. —
> The last time I put them by
> I was weary, like to die!

Following that scene, Agnes's husband requires her to give up every relic of her dead child. The few baby clothes she has kept must be handed over to a begging wretch who doesn't even know what man fathered her child in a ditch. With increasing anguish and then with "radiant happiness" Agnes turns over the clothes to the beggar woman and cries out:

> Robbed and rifled, even the last
> Tie that bound me to the past!
> I am free, Brand, free at last!

Apart from the theological message of the play (all or nothing), I think the point here is that if one goes all the way through the pain, into the worst of it, one comes out on the other side free. Maybe.

One woman called Joyce wrote me about the deaths of two of her very young children a year or so apart, from a genetic disease. Because of the family's financial plight, the two little ones were buried one on top of the other. A few years later, when circumstances were better, Joyce bought a headstone for the grave. "When I went to the cemetery to view the stone," she writes, "I was shocked by my reaction. It was as if I were overcome with a primitive desire to claw at the dirt with my bare hands, to get my children out of there."

I have a cousin whose older daughter was killed in a car accident more than twenty years ago and whose eyes still fill with tears when she speaks of Jan. I know several parents whose sons were killed in motorcycle fatalities who still cannot refer to the past event without present anguish. "We are changed forever by our loss," Joyce writes. All of us.

Thoughts that begin "If only . . ." are the worst foe. But for bad timing, a moment earlier or a moment later, but for an instant decision on the part of a physician or a paramedic or a police officer, but for a stupid miscalculation, but for any malevolent trick of Fate, the child might still be alive today. Death is so hard to live with. "Each day I have to face the truth again," another mother writes.

Kathy's son died in a boating accident, not by drowning, because he had a life jacket, but probably from hypothermia, because the police didn't look for him in time. She has been patient with and generous to her other sons and her husband as well as herself in the mourning process, being honest about her anger, making allowances for other modes of grieving than her own and — most astonishingly — discovering a paradox in the process. Two conflicting emotions can exist at the same time. In the course of the first year of her grief work, Kathy found that she and her husband, though they "still got into tangles," reached a better tolerance and understanding of each other's ways of handling their grief. This she acknowledged to be a blessing.

"Two truths can apply at the same time," she writes. "One, it is a blessing, and two, the cost is just too high." (It always is; unfortunately, no one has ever said when too much is enough.) The summer following Chris's death, Kathy saw her other two sons go off on a canoe trip with terrible trepidation. She realized that the trip was necessary, as a way for the two boys to deal with their brother's death. In spite of her own fears and anxieties, she let them go, wishing them a good time. "Again, two truths," she writes. "We were both very, very relieved to see the boys arrive safely back." Paradox is hard to live with, but how it stretches one!

If ever there is a case of unresolved grief, it occurs with the disappearance of a child. Juvenile or adult, a lost or runaway child strikes equal parts of terror and pain into a parent's heart. In the first days following the absence, hope collides with anger:

- "How could she be so stupid?"
- "If I get my hands on him, I'll teach him for running away."
- "He has never done anything so terrible before."

Then fear begins to overcome hope:

- "He must be alive; I'd know if he weren't, or would I?"
- "I didn't realize she was so unhappy."
- "Will I ever see him again?"

Little children get lost in the woods, are swept away by rain-swollen streams, abducted by strangers, and sometimes kidnapped by a divorced parent. Older children and teenagers run away from home (sometimes for legitimate reasons) and get hooked on drugs and take to the streets, or join a cult. When adult children disappear, the cause is seldom amnesia; more likely suicide or murder has taken them. With all the panic and anxiety flying around, there is another pain that doesn't occur in any other situation: not knowing.

Parents and loved ones are unable to close the file on a life that may or may not be over. Until the child shows up, dead or alive, doors stay open, self stays invested, love stays vulnerable. A parent moves into a limbo space where the child, a shadowy question mark, hovers forever — it seems like forever — until the final verdict. We all have good news and bad news. We read in the papers of the discovery of human remains and their subsequent identification. We read of sad — seldom triumphant — returns and humble capitulations. And we know personal stories that have happened to people we know: a fifteen-year-old girl who took off on some necessary odyssey, hitch-hiking, shooting up, "finding herself" (it looked more like getting hopelessly lost), and finally, after almost two years, returning to her family, not intact but able to go on. (She's thirty-something now, and a lively, contributing human being.) Then there was a young man in his late teens who obeyed his wanderlust for less than a year; he called his family and asked for a ticket home for Christmas; another unhappy young man simply disappeared, taking neither clothes nor money, and has never been seen again. Dead or gone? After nine years, his parents simply do not talk about him. The absence is like a radiation burn: it never closes, never heals.

What can be done with this kind of raw, unresolved grief? No pat answers are possible here, not that pat answers ever do any good, but people have the sense to realize how slick and empty and useless they are in cases like these. One is caught in a limbo, trapped like a fly in amber between past and future, with only the unknowable now. What comfort is there?

"Rest in the riddle." The line is from Christopher Fry's *The Lady's Not for Burning*, and it was an answer to an unanswerable question. There are, in fact, very few answers to the big questions we all stumble over. "I don't know" is one of the most common answers, and one that more parents should have the honesty to say to their children. Is there life after death? I don't know.

The fact is, there are no guarantees in life. Some situations make it easier for us to pretend there are, that's all. Whether we know it, are aware of it, or like it, we are all of us suspended in a kind of limbo, halfway between then and there, caught between now and somewhere. So rest in the riddle! I will try to be more specific.

Someone said to me when my husband died, "It's a good thing he went first because he couldn't have borne the pain of losing you," meaning it was better for me to bear the pain than for Bill. I know I wouldn't wish that pain on anyone. Perhaps that is one partial answer to the unanswerable pain of a loved one's unexplained disappearance: find meaning in the suffering. If it teaches tolerance and compassion, if it triggers action and leads to concern for others, then the suffering has meaning.

Parents whose child disappeared started a lost child association, a network that provides clues and assistance and encouragement to other "lost parents." Other people give long hours of volunteer service to crisis centers in the hope that a voice like theirs in another city somewhere might be available to their child in crisis. These people have discovered that the true meaning of suffering is not inside the psyche of the sufferer but out there in the world where suffering is transformed into action. We do not live in a closed system. We cannot survive if we remain closed. So we remain open to suffering and find meaning through it. This is the hardest lesson we have to learn. Ironically, the ones who learn it (or reject it) first are the ones who have this unbearable, open-ended pain: unresolved grief for a loved one whose fate is unknown.

When there is a death in the family, good things can come of it. If its members turn to each other for support and comfort, if they help each other to be weak and to grow by turns, if they treat the situation as an opportunity to search for more meaning in their own lives, then the child will not have died "in vain," as the saying goes. This is when living memorials can be a source of comfort, when the disease or event that carried off the child becomes a cause, a reason to get involved and to do battle so that others coming after may be saved. Such zeal often incites or spurs entire community movements: funding campaigns for research into the disease that caused the death, support groups and networks to deal with the pain leading up to and away from the death, the establishment of various means to try to prevent further deaths. Parents whose child has been murdered, for example, will ensure the creation of a good Block Parents Plan to provide sanctuary for a child threatened with rape or murder on the streets.

Parents of murder victims are not always vindictive. Few seem to hold with the eye-for-an-eye system of justice. What good would it do? Their child is still dead. What some parents prefer to do is see to it that such a horror cannot happen to another family. They require the imprisonment (but not the death sentence) of the murderer, but more important, they work for the safety of all children.

These are the most painful losses — murder and suicide. These are the deaths that truly do go against nature, and keep on causing agonizing grief years and years after the tragedy. If-only's and guilt are hard to put away.

- "If only I had listened to him."
- "If only I had realized how troubled she was."
- "If only I had been home."
- "If only I had picked her up at the bus stop."

Round and round, the painful thoughts and recriminations go, solving no problems but continually reliving errors. Parents are often devastated, and keep on being so.

"Having been," says Viktor Frankl, "is the surest kind of being." This is the essence of the psychiatrist's theory of what he calls "logo-therapy." There is no room for avoidance of suffering or evasion of pain here. We are not on earth, reasons Frankl, to pursue happiness, though most people in this century and on this continent seem to think so. In fact, one of the reasons for being unhappy is that people think they should be happier than they are. That's why Christmas gets a score of 12 in the Social Readjustment Rating Scale, because of the happiness gap — the discrepancy between expectations and reality. If not to be happy, then what?

If only one could see a meaning in one's life. When people clutch happiness, or the illusion of happiness, and deny suffering, they lose all sense of meaning. Therefore, it is a good thing for people to develop a *capacity for suffering*. That's why, in the case of an infant loss, touching and holding and gathering mementoes of the dead child is so valuable. By these acts, bereaved parents gain a sense of "having been." Having been. No one can take that kind of being away. That is the essence of self, of being — having been.

Statistics tell us that everyone suffers a loss through death on average every six years throughout adult life. Granted, sometimes deaths seem to cluster in a family, three or four in a year. As Shakespeare said, "When sorrows come, they come not single spy, but in battalions." But in between disasters, people are granted respite, some kind of emotional oasis when life and living seem "normal." What, indeed, is normal? *Suffering is normal*, according to psychiatrists, and we know that the acceptance of the challenge to suffer bravely is what gives life meaning up to its last moment. This, I think, is the supreme gift that Kübler-Ross gives to the dying (both children and adults) — the sense of the significance of one's individual life and one's own suffering.

From logotherapy to logodrama, Frankl offers an exercise: to imagine ourselves at eighty, looking back at our life from our deathbed. Such an act of imagination serves to remind us of our freedom of choice. We can see our turning-points. We cannot retract the past but we can make a decision about the next moment we live, and thus about the record of our future history.

Nothing can be undone, but the next thing can be different. Thus we can choose to rejoice that we had a child who was dear to us; we can be grateful that we knew each other for a while, however short it was. Of course, we grieve for the possibilities that still lay unrealized ahead of us, and wish there had been more time together, but we have the solid reality of the past, the time passed together, the love shared, the suffering bravely born. For that we can be grateful. The grieving goes on, but it is meaningful. Rest in the riddle.

11. Loss of a Life-Companion

We know, and must face it honestly, that life for us can never
be the same again.
—DAPHNE DU MAURIER, AND COUNTLESS OTHERS

WITH THE DEATH OF A LIFE-COMPANION, THE BOTTOM drops out of everything. The loss is so staggering that it seems impossible to resume anything like normal living again. The astonishing fact is that, once upon a time, before this shattered union, one was not half a couple, but whole. Where did that other whole person go? Can wholeness ever be reclaimed? Can the wound ever be healed?

In the spectrum of psychic pain, loss of a mate ranks as the most traumatic. What a wealth of human suffering is implicit in those words! Yet people do survive. At first, they act — react — as if death had no right to touch their lives, as if they were supposed to be immune. Then, after the shock, comes denial, anger, and depression, none so neatly compartmentalized or experienced in the working through as in the listing of them. Finally, most survivors achieve some sort of acceptance and begin to reorganize their lives. But the process I summarized in three sentences can take anywhere from a year or two to five, to forever, that is, the remainder of one's life, to complete. It's called going on alone, and it isn't easy.

Some, of course, do not go on alone, particularly men (25 percent of widowers remarry, as opposed to 1 percent of widows). Some, of course, take longer than others. Some, of course, take detours. Some, of course, die in the process. Looking at the whole picture from the plateau I am presently (and gratefully) standing on, I can see patterns emerging. I offer you now a compendium of clues I have followed on my way to discovering that grieving can be a creative process.

We had been at church on the morning of the day my husband died. It was Easter Sunday, and the sermon that morning was about how important it was that Jesus Christ had *lived*, not just that he had died. I kept writing that thought in the replies I wrote to the sympathy letters and I tried to hold onto it. It was important that my husband had lived. I was grateful for the relationship we had, and would continue to have.

One doesn't have to be a Christian to make this kind of discovery. Rabbi Earl Grollman, whose books and talks on grieving have been of such comfort to so many people, has some useful words for us. Claiming to be "six feet above contradiction" because he's a clergyman, Grollman reminds us that "grief is an emotion, not a disease. "Death," he says, "takes a life but it doesn't end a relationship; in spite of recovering, it's never over."

In any relationship, an emotional investment has been made; the withdrawal of it is necessarily painful. In any relationship where self has been committed to the care and well-being of another, the self must be recovered. Loss of self is the root of all loss, and the recovery and discovery of self are, I believe, the root of creation. Therefore, the grieving must be specific, conscious, careful, and goal-oriented. Above all, the grief work must be completed. Unresolved grief festers like an infection, ticks like a time bomb, swells like a tumor, and causes untold horror and pain later on when it bursts and destroys the organism that harbored it.

One younger widow called me four years after her husband's death. She was still dependent on the tranquilizers her doctor had prescribed for her while searchers were trying to recover the body after a fishing expedition. Without children or close family she had tried to carry on with her life as if nothing had happened. She had attended a wedding the night before she talked to me and she told me she had been shaken by a duty dance with her friend's husband — the first time she had been in a man's arms since her bereavement. Four or five crucial, unreleased (that is, undealt-with) time bombs blew up simultaneously in this woman's face: the sudden death of her husband that she had not yet come to terms with, her terror connected with the initial uncertainty about the body, her lack of a support system, her dependency on drugs, and her frustrated sexuality. The first thing she had to do, I told her, was to get off the drugs, the second was to find a human support system.

The perception is that widows have it harder than widowers. Men argue that this is not true; widowers are simply less visible (they hide more) than widows and less likely to ask for help. Men's mortality rate certainly increases, and they do have fewer social resources — at first. The consensus is that the first year is harder on widowers and the second year harder on widows. Statistics tell us that widowers remarry within eighteen months of bereavement, on average — or die — while those who are still alive and single say this is a myth. The moral is that no one has a corner on pain.

We all tend to think of conventionally mated and bereaved pairs, forgetting other equally devoted liaisons. What about live-in relationships, and what about long-term homosexual and lesbian commitments? Young or old, suddenly or slowly, the loved ones who leave us create a hole in our lives. The fact is that the loss of a life-companion under any circumstances is a tough one to endure. I have this image of a child's sticker book with white spaces for the colored stickers to be pasted in to complete the picture. When someone we love dies, we are left with these white spaces, an incomplete picture, no color, and no stickum.

We see only the empty space and the hole we've been left in. At a time like this, no one can convince us to be grateful, and I caution sympathizers to avoid that kind of sententious, unhelpful comfort: "You have your (choose one or more): health, children, memories, money." None of these is adequate compensation for what we have lost. But one widow who wrote me gave me an idea I hadn't thought of: "Death always leaves us aware of what we perceive ourselves to have missed, but we've no way of knowing what we have been spared. . . . When [my husband] was dying, I found myself writing to a friend, 'I can't even pray for mercy, because for all we know we are in the midst of a miracle of mercy, and lack only the heightened understanding and clarity of vision to recognize it.' "

It takes more than clarity of vision for a bereaved life-companion to withdraw from a union that was less than perfect. Where there were unresolved conflicts, deep misunderstanding, even bitter resentment, the survivor has trouble letting go. There was more to say, on both sides; neither one has had a full say. The end didn't round off a life, it simply cut short an argument. People who are thus denied as well as bereaved find themselves more angry than those who emerge from happier relationships. They want to keep on fighting.

Another odd phenomenon occurs. We all know the Pedestal Syndrome, putting one's departed mate on a pillar out of reach of ordinary mortals, like children or would-be suitors or lovers. It's very hard to walk in the footsteps of someone on a pedestal. The bereaved who are most guilty of this posthumous idealization are usually the ones who had the least happy liaisons. *De mortuis nil nisi bonum*, as the Latin proverb goes, but saying nothing but good about the dead and outright lying about their saintly qualities are two different things. Another form of ambivalence has taken shape before our very eyes. Are we talking about the same person?

When a woman emerges from a traditional marriage, she has to rediscover her autonomy, foster her sense of self, and, above all, develop her ability to nurture herself. One of the most painful lessons I had to learn, and it was literally *years* after my husband died (fourteen, to be exact), was that *I was not Number One in anyone's life*. It had taken a long time for that knowledge to sink in. Perhaps the realization comes more quickly to someone who does not have dependent children living with her at the time she is bereaved. Other widows (and divorcées) have similar delayed reactions, though. I know this because, when I tell them my "discovery," I can see they are as startled and pained as I was. However, when I spoke of it to a never-married woman, she nodded comfortably. "Of course," she said, with no hesitation and no surprise. How else could it be? I must have been simple-minded not to have known that. I was.

One could go on to question whether one really was number one at any time; I suppose it depends on the marriage. An unspoken covenant exists in most marriages in our time: in return for devoting one's life to the well-being of another and of the children (if any) of the union, a woman will be *needed*, important, loved, and taken care of for life. The death of the spouse wipes out the agreement, and she may be left with very little; the average insurance settlement on a widow is about $15,000.

115

This accounts for the number of elderly single women (44 percent of them) living below the poverty level.

Once my shocking discovery has struck home, and this number-preference system discarded, self-discovery and self-nurturing can proceed. They had better, because there is no one else in sight. Thus widows begin to grow on their own. They have to.

One other aspect of the process might be considered, another idea that shocked and even repelled some of the first people I tried it out on. In Act IV of George Bernard Shaw's play *The Doctor's Dilemma*, Dubedat, an unprincipled poet (whose life, the doctors decide, must not be saved in order to preserve an inaccurate memory of his finer qualities), is instructing his wife on his deathbed. He tells her how he wants to be mourned:

> *If there's one thing I hate more than another, it's a widow. Promise me that you'll never be a widow . . . I want you to look beautiful. I want people to see in your eyes that you were married to me . . . I want them to point at you and say, 'There goes a woman who has been in heaven.' — If you wear black and cry, people will say, 'Look at that miserable woman: her husband made her miserable.' . . . Promise me you will not make a little hell of crape and crying and undertaker's horrors and withering flowers and all that vulgar rubbish.*

This is an approach to grieving that I welcome. People, mainly discontented wives, have often said to me, on viewing my career since my husband's death, that they *envy* me. My explanation has something of Dubedat's philosophy in it. My husband was a fascinating, witty man, exciting to live with, and always unexpected, even after twenty years together. I decided early on, in the first bleak year of bereavement, when I certainly wasn't having any fun, that my life had damn well better be interesting or I wasn't having any of it. I proceeded to try to fill it, to take on challenges I didn't know whether I could handle, to rush into experiences I wasn't always certain I would survive, to get to know people I would never even have met, and, no matter what, to say yes to life. I lured myself on, made my life livable, and thereby honored my husband's memory. Thus, my emergence as a butterfly from the chrysalis of my grief was directly related to my widowhood and was in no way intended as a negative commentary on my marriage.

Survival is essential; we must be agreed on that. Death is not a solution to bereavement. Although the recently bereaved experience more hospital admissions than the general population and have a higher death rate, most of us do go on (reluctantly) living. "I'm tired of people saying life goes on," one widow said to me. "I never gave it permission."

A friend of mine who quit smoking said he finally got the hang of it when he realized that smoking was a gesture and that if he analyzed the relationship of the smoking gesture to what else he was doing, he could use that discernment to eliminate the gestures. I understood immediately. Four of the best cigarettes of my life were after the birth of each child, when I could finally relax. I stopped having children and, right away, there went one smoking gesture! (Bear with me; this is not as facetious as it sounds.) My friend said that, as he discovered his associations with cigarettes, he rethought them, sidestepped them, did other things. For example, instead of sitting down to make a phone call and automatically lighting a cigarette while he waited to make the connection and talk, he stood up to phone, or sat in a different chair, or took a pencil in his hand to make notes on the ensuing conversation, thereby eliminating his smoking gesture.

We live with familiar gestures. We also love with familiar gestures. We make habits of our gestures and our loving. "Where love is concerned it is easier to renounce a feeling than give up a habit," said Proust. I suggest that, as part of the process of grieving, we have to lose a habit, that is, to eliminate our familiar gestures. Of course, it is impossible to eliminate them all. (If one did, one would be dead.) Each simple gesture of walking (alone now), eating (alone now), going to bed (alone now), and so on, must be rethought, restructured, relearned.

Walking: I walked in different directions, at different times. Sometimes I found companions to walk with, but no regulars. I know a widow who took up cross-country skiing to replace walking with her husband, and who joined a club with regular group outings. I know a widower who bought a bicycle and found women bikers to make picnics for him. I read of a widower who bought tons of camping equipment and an all-terrain vehicle — an expensive way to replace his walking wife!

Eating: However much one may become accustomed to being alone, eating alone has to be the most recurrent problem; it happens three times a day. For a time I tried cooking for others, but that didn't work;

few of them returned my invitations. Eating at home, I listen to music, read, park in a chair in front of the TV, picnic somewhere away from the dining table. Eating out, traveling, I deliberately take dinner flights on planes and talk to my seatmate, I ask for special care in good dining rooms (on expenses), and jot things in my journal, or I take a book to McDonald's and pay no attention to the food or the surroundings.

Going to bed: "There is no sanctuary in one bed from the memory of another," said Cyril Connolly. For the warmth I need in bed, no longer supplied by another warm body, I rely on my duvet at home, or socks and a sweater in strange beds (friends' and hotels'). Warm milk (with a drop of vanilla or brandy) releases a natural sedative (I can spell it: tryptophan). A book puts some to sleep, but I'll stay up and finish it, thereby eliminating not only the gesture but sleep as well. Music, a fire (I have a beautiful fireplace now), my journal — all these now woo me to bed, in lieu of a husband. Best of all is my journal.

I have substituted an addictive gesture for most of the gestures associated with my lost love. Where once I took all my confidences and gossip, my worries and my plans, my casual chat and serious discussions to my husband, I take them now to my journal. I recommend such a gesture, if only for a short time. For some, as for me, it may turn out to be the continuing and habitual gesture of a lifetime.

Anne Philipe, the widow of the French film actor Gerard Philipe, kept a journal after her husband's death. The "you" in her diary is not herself or the diary persona, it is her husband. "Sometimes I resent you for being dead," she writes. It took her a while to admit that "there was nothing to be expected of you . . . you were absent from my world forever." She decided that she wanted to save herself, "not deliver myself from you."

There it is again — the self that must be saved. A journal is an effective method of recovery, personal, flexible, available, and even, as I say, addictive. In time, in a way, the journal becomes the surrogate companion. It has become so for me. Nothing has happened, not officially, nothing is real until I record it; I can't seem to sort out my day, let alone my life, until I have written everything down, even, sometimes, what I ate, when I showered, whom I phoned, where I shopped, what I bought. I have substituted one habit for another. I recommend it. The very banality of everyday activities thus recorded offers a reassuring handle on normalcy to a bereaved or lonely person. We all, as Kierkegaard says, "tranquilize ourselves with the trivial." The trivial can be very comforting. Recording the trivial, that is, journal-writing, is a comforting gesture.

In the early days of my grief, I didn't always wait until evening to confide in my journal. Often an encounter or a discovery would drive me to it during the day. I remember one such time. I had heard a song on the radio: "I can't live, if living is without you." The words were stupid but they were so patently untrue they hurt and angered me. There I was, living without my love and, against my will, still living. I wrote down what I was feeling, blotted the page (tears not ink), and went on with my bleak day.

Survivors keep returning to that implacable fact. We are still living *without* the person who gave reason to our living, as well as illumination and significance. Now we have to find a new reason, new light, and new meaning. How can we do that when we can scarcely think, have no appetite, spend sleepless nights, and can barely trust people, let alone life? It seems impossible.

"I must be doing it wrong." Survivors say that when the grief remains so sharp, with no respite. No one ever told them it would last this long. Society has denied us this certainty about grief now, and denied us its full expression. We're supposed to look better, to be coming round, taking it well, as if we're coping, as if we're getting over it. We're supposed to "get on with it." What is *it*? Life, I think.

A widow told me recently that people keep instructing her to get on with it. "I *am* getting on with it," she said. "Grieving is part of getting on with it. Tell people that." I'll try.

I discovered early on and have been saying it ever since that grief is hard work, and very tiring. Other bereaved people notice this tiredness, and the amount of energy drained off by grief. In his book about grief, *A Grief Observed*, C.S. Lewis called it inertia — a complete lack of will or strength to do anything beyond the bare essentials. Some people in their grief sleep all the time, every chance they get, round the clock if they could. Others, like me, find sleep irrelevant, and exist only through forced cat-naps. Lack of sleep, however, does not account for the bone-weariness. It's the grieving process itself that saps the marrow from one's bones, the spring from one's step, the hope from one's soul. Some people, again like me, can't eat (the only time I ever get thin is when

I'm desperately unhappy); my throat seizes up, my stomach turns off at the sight of food. Others, like another widow whose journal I found, turn to ice cream and custard and chocolate — her favorite comfort foods — and gain weight.

This woman, M.T. Dohaney, a writer herself, is yet another widow who has turned to a journal as part of her recovery therapy. She records in a personal diary her reactions during the first year following her husband's death, and confirms, if one needs the confirmation, the wild, desperate range of emotions a survivor staggers through, with no guidelines, but with the help of a few very supportive friends. The title of the book is *When Things Get Back to Normal* — deliberately and well chosen. As Dohaney says, "I have to accept the fact that life will never again go back to normal, or at least to my perception of normal. For today at least, normal is pain and I have to learn to accept that."

Normal is pain. Ay, there's the rub.

In the earliest days of pain and bewilderment, the old Straw-Clutching Syndrome comes into heavy play. Whatever tiny happening offers a glimmer of hope becomes the Event of the Day. A new flower in the garden, a new moon, a pattern of frost on the window, a cup of coffee with a friend, a hug from same — or from one's child, or parent? — someone, something, anything that eases the present pain for a few moments, these are the straws that save us from drowning. I used to compare the moments to beads on a string, these instances relatively free from pain. They were brief and infrequent at first, and I used to take conscious note of them when they occurred.

"Right now is all right," I'd say. "Now is okay. I can bear now."

Little by little the nows added up, until I could put a few of them together for an hour, a couple of hours, a day, a week, until my "beads" were numerous enough to make a necklace. Laughter was like that too. I collected laughs. "Move a muscle," says Alcoholics Anonymous (I am told), "and the mind will follow." Laughter uses a number of muscles that fall into disuse after the death of a life-companion. One has to look for reasons to laugh first. Sometimes it's a difficult search. I discovered that most of my supporters were no help in this regard. They didn't make me laugh. Well-meaning friends tended to tell me hard-luck stories of other people in worse straits than I was, to remind me that I wasn't so badly off and that I should be grateful.

Norman Cousins had the right idea (in *Anatomy of an Illness*) when, in illness, he turned to old Laurel and Hardy movies to make him laugh and thus relax enough to sleep without a sedative. Old comedies and young children are a good source of laughter. Kids are unconscious comedians and often make us laugh — or, if not laugh, then smile. If the children are close to us, the smiles are very sweet and lift the heart as well as the mouth.

A pocketful of wry helps too, a sense of irony and of one's self as a conscripted clown in the circus of life. I like this line (it's called an Irish bull) and I use it often when I encounter something outrageous: "If my husband were alive today, he'd turn over in his grave." I enjoy in a weird way some of the boners people pull in their less tactful moments; in fact, I collect them.

- "Isn't it lucky your husband died when he did? Otherwise you'd have been too old to start a second career." Very lucky.
- "It must be wonderful to be so free, to go where you want and come home when you want with no one waiting impatiently for you to return and wanting to know where you've been." Hard-won freedom, though, and I still brace myself for the silence of re-entry.
- "You've got everything, haven't you?" What does one say to that? Elizabeth Taylor says, "I haven't had tomorrow." That's a pretty good answer.

Wry humor doesn't necessarily produce outright laughter, but a wry and watery smile can offer a detached perspective on one's new situation: "Whoever thought that I, (choose one or more) protected wife; loving husband; faithful companion; passionate lover; skillful, logical, competent, placid human being, would end up (choose one or more) grovelling on my knees? shrieking in rage? whimpering with pain? cowering in fear? blundering in the dark? making love with another person?"

No, it's not enough to make one laugh but it does make one grin at Fate. Laugh, goes the old saying, and the world laughs with you; cry, and you cry alone.

Alone isn't so bad. Deep down we know we are alone. We are born alone, die alone, even if in the company of others. Everyone knows that. Alone — we can stand that. It's *lonely* that does us in.

"I'm scared of being alone," writes one widower, "of not having anyone."

And another says, "I get lonely when there's no one around."

A widow writes, in simple anguish, "I am so very lonely."

The empty, echoing space a widow cannot but must endure is not simple loneliness. She has been hollowed out with her pain and loss and there is no security, no comfort. Other people cannot fill this void. Oddly enough, survivors of happy marriages don't always want it to be filled.

Indeed, when a secure attachment is broken by death, the recovery of the survivor, though difficult (and involving the recovery of self), is still not as tough as it is for those whose unions were more troubled and less empathetic. Those people whose dialogue was incomplete must seek to finish what was left undone and unsaid before they can get on with the rest of their grief work. Good strong attachments that end with death have laid a foundation for the skill of solitude. It's not really sudden, though the transition may be abrupt.

Loneliness remains the biggest, most painful problem that the bereaved have to face, especially those who have lost their life-companion. In addition, they have usually lost their best friend, severest critic, wisest counselor, kindest mentor, and most devoted serf.

I used to call my marriage "mutual serfdom." Where else, in this day and age, could one have a helper at one's (each other's) beck and call? I becked, he called, and vice versa. The loneliness that follows the loss of such loving care, friendly support, and happy companionship is simply overwhelming. Loneliness is the real cause of grief unending. Loneliness gouges the bedrock, and it never stops. Sometimes it stops, for a time, for some people, if they marry again, but they know, deep inside, what's waiting for them in the shadows. What we have to do is learn how to be lonely. To do that we have to get reacquainted with our self. We will, soon.

12. Loss of Self

Only what is really oneself has the power to heal.
— CARL JUNG

"LAWK-A-MERCY ON ME, THIS IS NONE OF I!" THE OLD nursery rhyme inspired me to write a children's play (*The Old Woman and the Pedlar*), but of course it wasn't the rhyme that caused it, it was my Life Event. The Old Woman in the story fell asleep by the side of the road on her way home from the market, and "along came a pedlar/And his name was Stout,/And he cut her petticoats all round about/And she began to shiver/And she began to shake" and she looked down (she'd probably never seen her legs before) and said "Lawk-a-mercy [Lord have mercy] on me, this is none of I!" Even her dog didn't know her. My play begins there. It's a search for identity as the old woman seeks help to find out who she is since she's not herself any more.

Just as the Old Woman decides that her search is hopeless, an adenoidal, unbearably optimistic games mistress–type called Hope enters to try to reassure her and give her some hope to cling to.

"What's wrong?" Hope asks the Old Woman.

"Well, you see," says the Old Woman, "I thought I knew who I was and where I was going."

"Who *are* you and where *are* you going?" asks Hope.

This children's play opened during the same week that my book *Beginnings* (a book for widows) was published. I hadn't realized it, but my director pointed out the fact to me, that I ask the same questions in both works:

> You're alone now. You're you. Who are you? And where are you going? What do you want? If you think I'm asking tough questions, you're right. I've been asking myself the same ones.
> — BEGINNINGS: A BOOK FOR WIDOWS

The search for identity, that is, for self, goes on, at whatever level we conduct it. The cry comes so frequently from the bereaved that it seems to be another one of the scripted responses, not original at all, but universal and heartfelt:

- "I am lost."
- "I don't know who I am any more."
- "I've lost my self."
- "Who am I?"
- "I feel so helpless and lost."
- "I have not only lost my husband, I have lost everything good, and I have lost myself."

This is what loss and change are really all about. The death of people dear to us, the death of a relationship, causes profound changes that shake the underpinnings, the foundation of our existence. They threaten our sense of self.

We thought we knew who we were. But, when we take away the qualifiers — child of so-and-so, mate of so-and-so, parent of so-and-so, of some more or less fixed address, some sort of stated purpose, and a more or less comfortable persona — what's left? Who are we? Where are we going? We have lost our self. How do we get it back?

All our lives, our selves have been invested in what we do, what we care for. We pledge allegiance, we sign contracts, we plight our troth, we commit our love. With each promise we give a piece of ourselves into another's keeping, in return, of course, for certain rights and privileges. Belonging to a country, to a cause and institutions, to a family and to loved ones gives us a sense of purpose and, above all, of self. When any one of these roots is pulled from us, we feel the tug and the loosening. When the taproot goes, that is, our mate, then we are in real danger. As the psychologists tell us, this is the reason that the loss of the life-companion is still highest on the SRRS stress chart. Why?

Ideally, we grow separately, yet frequently a person's life can be so entwined in another's that when one life stops, the other life is threatened. The poet Kahlil Gibran warns us of this in his poem *The Prophet*:

> And stand together yet not too near together:
> For the pillars of the temple stand apart,
> And the oak tree and the cypress grow not in each
> other's shadow.

When two people grow in each other's shadow and one of them dies, the other one, lacking that shelter, almost dies as well. It is for this reason that friends and a support system are so valuable: they provide a little shade.

The bereaved requires a sense, first, of security, then, of continuity. Widowers tend to find a substitute as quickly as they can, to replace the departed one, thereby restoring the security, and the shelter. Widows, in contrast, find out who they are after all these years. They find they can grow in that glaring sunlight.

No matter what means is sought for the alleviation of pain and eventual recovery, the process is slow and painful. No matter how lightly or deeply the self was invested in the life of another person, the departure of the other causes withdrawal symptoms. The self is like a foot that has been frozen or fallen asleep. As feeling and circulation are restored, the foot hurts. The emergence from the suspended state causes heightened sensitivity. One's nerve ends are too acute for comfort. So, when self emerges from a suspended state, perhaps anesthetized all these years, certainly immersed in another's well-being, scarcely answerable to its owner, awakened, self is like Rip van Winkle after a sleep of ten? twenty? fifty? years, alien and lost. It needs a crash course in the present.

People can be shaken by a loss that does not necessarily strip them from their moorings. A man who lost his closest friend was thus forcibly reminded of his own mortality. He finally started making some effort to quit smoking, lose weight, take regular exercise, and look after himself in some kind of startled, belated bid for longevity. Fear prompted this change, not loss of self. Soon lulled into indifference again, the man slipped back into his old habits.

I know any number of people, including me, whose good intentions were not carried out until someone's death made them irrelevant, and who changed their ways with others after that: they write the note, send the flowers, deliver the baking, run the errand, do the favor without procrastinating because tomorrow may be too late. Surely we have all noted such changes in someone we know. Activated by loss, this kind of change is not really a change but merely a shift. The altered behavior is just that — an alteration.

The If-you-knew-you-were-going-to-die-tomorrow game has a catalytic effect on the emotions. What misunderstanding would you like to clear up? With whom would you like to make peace? Whom would you ask to forgive you? To whom would you want to express your love, hitherto unspoken or not repeated often enough, before you die? These are still superficial compared to the profound changes caused by the loss of self.

A parable: someone is supposed to have gone to St. Francis when he was planting onions and asked him what he would do if he knew he was going to die tomorrow. "Go on planting onions," was the saint's reply.

Thus people do — or do not — change their lifestyle to a greater or lesser extent when forced by a loss to evaluate their own lives and relationships. But these are still superficial changes. The deeper change occurs with the withdrawal of the emotional investment in another person, that is, the withdrawal of self. In contrast to the fresh leaves encouraged by the bright light illuminating the surviving tree, the roots of self burrow more deeply. Self must go underground, at least for a while. It does not change — yet. That takes more time, time and a creative grieving process.

To have lost one's mate sounds as if a casual aberration or a mere misplacement has occurred (which is why I prefer to say *die, dead, death* instead of "passed away," "departed," "eternal slumber," and "final rest"). To lose one's self, is shattering. Without self there is no I to be, no I/eye to focus, no center core to stabilize one's life. All our lives, our relationships keep changing. Perception alters, values shift, attention wanders, and purpose wavers. One must restore stability if one is to go on living in this world. The core of our being, the essence of our humanity must be recovered. A reminder: recovery does not mean the end of pain.

There are two ways in which one can lose self. The first way, through the death of a mate or child, can snap all the moorings and hurl the bereaved out of a comfortable role and unquestioned status. This loosening of ties is what people really mean when they say, "I don't know who I am any more." If they make their tortuous way to autonomy and authenticity, they will understand what widows mean when they read from the Universal Script, "Isn't it ironic that I had to lose my husband in order to find myself?"

The other way to lose self is even more frightening because it is irrevocable, and there are no rewards at the end of the line. That is the loss of self due to a debilitating, self-erasing disease such as Alzheimer's. In this case, the self must say goodbye to self and loved ones while there is still awareness. With no connection to past or future, and with a fading present, life asks questions no one can answer, certainly not the victim of such a disease but not the loved ones, either. Where is the creativity of survival in a life that can't be remembered or identified, let alone examined? Alzheimer's, said one victim, "is worse than death — it's unnatural. It's the end of hope."

But it is not the end of love. There is still feeling and communication, and there is *the present moment*, which is all any of us has. No one has any guarantee of tomorrow. Now is what we all have. We must learn to use it well. We would spare our loved one pain; spare ourselves, too, if we could. The real horror comes later when the other is buried in a living body; the blessing is that the victim is spared consciousness of that final ignominy. Since the self is lost, it is not there to know it is lost. Some people — most of us — feel that life is not life without consciousness, and consciousness not meaningful without memory. Erase memory and we are like a computer with its data bank stripped — useless. And yet, and yet . . .

The great neurologist A.R. Luria argues that we do not consist of memory alone. We have "feeling, will, sensibilities, moral being" — all things, we note, that cannot be examined, scanned, photographed, pasted in an album, or dissected. We also have — sorry, some may leave me over this — a *soul*. Self-less, the soul still exists, though suspended in an abyss of nothingness; self-less, the spirit can be absorbed in a spaceless, timeless present. Alzheimer's is the ultimate in existential disease; let us learn from it. Let us make allowances for the minute-by-minute integration of the human spirit in a continuum of love.

I want to return to the self that goes underground when someone dies. This self, whose yesterdays were buried with the dead and whose tomorrows are consciously dreaded, is the lost one who must search for meaning in the grieving process. The tools of survival must be at hand.

The role with which self has previously been associated has been destroyed. That does not mean there is no identity left. We just have to redefine it. Perhaps as never before, life offers us an opportunity to see our selves clearly, without the usual masking qualifications: someone's spouse, companion, parent, friend, employee, or employer. Thus stripped, the self can be re-evaluated. When the Old Woman in my play complained to Hope that she didn't know who she was, Hope asked her: "Who do you want to be?" Good answer.

Sometimes, somewhere along the way, we can lose sight of our assignment as well as our role. Losses that force the redefinement of a role frequently clarify the assignment — or offer a new one. Parents bereaved by murder invest themselves heavily in Block Parents programs to ensure the safety of other children; widows left lonely and stranded launch support groups to help others like themselves; PLWAs and their families campaign for hospices and greater tolerance. Death often seems to present new tasks to the survivors.

Suffering is the tool we would avoid if we could. Suffering offers the cutting edge of the grieving process, gouging out the insensitive, dead tissue, forcing us to new levels (depths) of pain, enabling us to feel compassion for others as never before. "There is nothing we can do with suffering except to suffer it," says C.S. Lewis. Grim words for a tool that is painful to use. We must grasp the untenable handle, bear the unbearable, endure the unendurable — in short, suffer — for it is only by facing the unavoidable and bowing to the inexorable that self learns the meaning of suffering, of life, and of death.

"I can't, I can't stand it. I can't go on." The protest comes from the heart, claiming weakness as a reason not to suffer any longer. But one older widow told me that, as her life went on, with its Life Events and the kind of pain that most of us suffer, sooner or later, she realized that her weakness was her strength. She staggered, she complained, she declared herself incapable of continuing, and she continued. "After a while," she said, "I knew I could go on, because I had." Farther in and farther on.

The burden we carry can be a source of strength. Even if it's heavier than we would like, we can develop muscles to make the carrying easier.

Fitness enthusiasts put weights on their wrists and ankles to increase the stress on their muscles, not because they wallow in pain but because they want to expand their capacity. My yoke is easy, and my burden light, Someone said. Self proves it by carrying it.

Grace is the tool that suffering hones. All the people who wrote me when I was writing this book demonstrate that quality, a rare combination of compassion, charity, mercy, and humility.

- "I find generally that I keep the grief in a special space in my mind."
- "I know that I am only one of thousands who share these traumas in life."
- "I have been, and remain, a woman richly blessed."
- "Some have stories far more complicated than mine — far more painful than mine. What's important is that . . . they should be told, so we can all reach out when we feel so desperate to be heard."
- "It is strange how we, or some of us, can eventually walk away alone quite contented, from a person who was once so very dear in our lives."

A definition of guts in my day was "intestinal fortitude" — courage, the ability to walk through the valley of the shadow of death, the underground where self must find self again, in order to carry on. Without this tool, there is no recovery because the attempt will never be made. The tool that forces the decision, though, is equally necessary: choice.

I will discuss choice at greater length, but not as a tool of the grieving process. We know, self knows, that we cannot always control what happens to us, cannot choose our destiny. This survival tool of choice cannot twist fate or turn off pain like a plumber's wrench. It can, however, change our perspective, strengthen our intention. "Intentional living," a phrase by Anonymous (who Virginia Woolf thought must have been a woman) expresses this choice mostly clearly. One can express an intention to live, one can choose to go on living. I am tense, I said in one of my poems, "tense, but present." Choosing to continue to be present at one's life is making good use of the tool of choice.

Thus the self has unlimited use of the tools of survival in the grieving process. Still, the way is not easy. "I feel so alone." There's another line from the Universal Script. Solitude holds terror for the self who has lost, not consciousness, but meaning. What's going to become of self (me)?

Self has to be reinvented. That is where the act of creation comes into play, the creativity that I maintain can be a positive corollary of grief.

Not many people are creative, at least not in the artistic sense of the word. Marshall McLuhan predicted a time when we would *all* be artists. He was talking about interaction, mutual communication; I'm talking about genuine creation. Unlike paintings, or musical compositions, or books, some creative acts don't last long enough to be perceived as creative acts: a tastefully balanced and cooked dinner, an aesthetically planned and planted garden, a harmoniously designed and furnished home. These domestic works of art usually do not linger past the life of their creators. (Madame Pompadour was a decorator; none of her interior designs remains.) Neither does a knowledge of tropical fish as evidenced in the fish tank, a passion for orchids seen in the greenhouse, an expertise with baseball, an aptitude for juggling or Monopoly. And what about human relationships? Some people are good with people. They may live in others' memories for a time but they do not last as long as words in books or paintings in a gallery — or do they?

We all prize achievement but we overlook excellence. We honor those who broaden our horizons and forget those who made us feel comfortable with them. I offer this brief argument by way of expanding the definition of creativity. Ordinary people give us glimpses of creation; an unsung, unhonored act of creation is valuable too. If it were not so, I would have to deny my grandmother, and we would all forget the shirts ironed (before Perma-Press), the kites strung, the wells dug, the food grown and cooked by all our ancestral creators.

As I say, there are different kinds of creation. What I am gradually working up to is the discovery that an enforced solitude, though painful at first, can actually teach us to create a new self. Once its strengths are appreciated, the self may develop a greater capacity for solitude. Some people, ordinary people, even reach the point where they consciously and actively seek out solitude. Everyone needs time alone.

One learns to develop what I call the skill of solitude (another tool). It is hard-won, this ability to be *alone*. It takes muscles that have to be toned, and flexibility and a willingness to talk to oneself without fear of insanity. Some people learn solitude early, by circumstances: lonely only children, children bereft of companionship by too many moves, by poverty, wealth, divorce, or the death of one or both parents. Others gravitate to solitude instinctively, by their nature. We tend to compartmentalize children these days, plunking them into their peer groups in day-care centers, schools, programs, camps, and so on, expecting them to get along and make friends.

Most of us know that it's quite possible to feel alone in a crowd, to be more lonely, in fact, in the company of a group of people with whom we have nothing in common than when alone. Isolation does not consist merely of physical removal from other human beings. People react differently to loneliness. Some seem never to accept it. They surround themselves with other people, not necessarily friends or intimates, simply voices to keep silence at bay or bodies to keep them warm. I may be accused of chauvinistic generalization here but it has been my observation that women tend to seek voices, and men bodies. This difference between widow and widower may serve as a caution to people dealing with them. Each is looking for something different to assuage his or her loneliness. When widow and widower turn to each other, they should be aware of that. I have observed, however, that second marriages are usually very successful when both parties are widowed and have waited long enough to recognize their needs.

There are other means than marriage to cope with loneliness. Some people throw themselves into their work or into good works and keep so busy there's no time to be lonely. Just one flaw here: there is always time to be lonely. *Time* is what people who have been left alone have the most of. I remember saying to myself over and over again, "I have all the time in the world," and I did. Even when time seems filled with appointments and activities, the grieving person has a constant underlying sense of space–time and of the endless time one's companion has fallen into from the moment of death. Two sets of time run concurrently in the survivor's head: earth time and eternal time. Even when busy and occupied in earth time, the bereaved feel at loose ends in eternity, not very safe, and quite lonely.

In a developing child we note with approval the increasing attention span, the ability to entertain oneself. We should also provide the opportunity for and note with similar approval the growing capacity to be alone.

This capacity is one of the sure signs of emotional maturity. Certainly, creativity is impossible without it. One needs empty wells of loneliness to fill with one's own thoughts and dark caverns of solitude to light with one's own illumination.

We keep forgetting that solitude enables us to learn more about ourselves, about others, and about the world we inhabit. We can develop such insights only if we have time to ourselves. We simply put in time with most other people; we *live* with ourselves. People, noise, distractions send up too much of a barrier between our external and internal worlds. Silence and solitude clear the path to the inner sanctum. Eventually we may be led to wisdom; ultimately we might find God, in whatever form He/She/It chooses to be found.

Many people these days hesitate to name this power God. I will not force a name (or denomination) on the Common Denominator of us all. God within, God without, by whatever name is comfortable, the healing function is discovered in solitude. Such healing, first of self, then of others, is the deep creative response of grief to the unanswerable question death asks. Rest in the riddle.

We all must experience the loss of and the discovery of self (we must, though not all of us do). Self is the ultimate product of the grieving process, awaiting every person who goes through the valley of pain. Every loss or change in life threatens our sense of self to a greater or lesser degree. Once we have discovered who our selves are, we can never be so threatened again, for we can re-create our selves as the need arises. It does keep arising, unfortunately.

V

DEATH OF A ROLE

*Death imperils one's world and the roles assigned in it.
Grieving enlarges to encompass the full loss.*

13. Loss of Self-Image

*When one is a stranger to oneself then one is estranged
from others too.*
—ANNE MORROW LINDBERGH

WHAT DIFFERENCE IS THERE, IT MIGHT BE ASKED, BETWEEN
self and self-image? I have already discussed the self in its many aspects:
the emotional investment that has to be recovered when a life-companion
dies, the consciousness that disappears with the deterioration of a mind,
the physical entity that departs this life in death. Self-image is different
again from all these selves; it, too, takes a beating when death occurs—
someone else's death, or the death of a relationship.

We have discussed some of the physical losses that accompany death:
loss of appetite, loss of sleep, loss of friends and associates. Financial
straits often force the loss of home and the lessening of material possessions, thereby involving the loss of roots and social connections. All these
losses challenge one's sense of self but it is the central loss of the person
that changes one's role and undermines one's self-image.

"Who did you used to be?" Older people get asked that when they
retire. (Answer: I still am. It takes a while to realize it, that's all.) Work
roles aren't the only ones from which one is retired. A wife (typically)
can be traded in for a newer model, as in the case of the mid-life dump
(divorce after forty-five), although "irreconcilable differences" can cause
as traumatic a loss of role for a male or female of any age. The death of
a child does not necessarily take away the function of parent if there are

surviving siblings, but it changes the role, nonetheless. The death of a spouse, mate, life-companion, of course, is the most profound change of all, if the relationship was one that gave both people their definition and meaning in life. The loss of any role inevitably causes a change of habits and lifestyle, frequently of location, and of familiar methods of doing things, certainly of comfortable assumptions, and ultimately of one's entire personality. (Lawk-a-mercy on me, this is none of I.) We have to adapt.

Alvin Toffler calls a person's adaptive mechanism the orientation response. He says one's orientation response is "particularly stressing when a novel event or fact challenges one's whole preconceived world view" — in other words, one experiences shock. Shock is the first defense mechanism thrown up in the face of loss. By our symptoms ye shall know us.

The "novel event," in this case, is a new role, and it's not just the world view that is challenged, it's the view of one's self, that is, one's self-image. We *are* what we do. When we do something different, we become different people. ("I used to be the egg lady. . . .") Thus we lose our earlier role.

It can happen with age, or with (or without) money. Suddenly, people call you "Sir" or "Madame" or, conversely, "Hey, you." Surnames are in, or first names are used without a reciprocal privilege. Most of us spend at least forty hours a week playing the role by which we are called. When the roll is called up yonder (I cannot resist puns), by what name will we be called? Who are we?

That question arises so frequently and with such anxiety among bereaved people that it has become part of the Universal Script.

- "I don't know who I am any more."
- "If I am no longer my daughter's mother, who am I?"
- "I have not only lost my husband, I have lost everything good, and I have lost myself."
- "You can't just say that you lost a spouse, that's not saying enough. You've lost a lot of things. You've lost a companion, an ego builder, you've lost a counselor who will tell you when you're right or when you're wrong. You've lost all of that. And you have to name what you've lost. I was also retired, and retirement is a loss to grieve too."

A retired man said to me recently that he couldn't understand the dread people had of retirement; it presented no losses to him. Yes, well, the man has a more-than-adequate income, a wife, his health, opportunities to travel, and several titles. He's still Mister, and not only do people know who he is, he does too. Most middle-income people who retire have few of those pluses now. (Lower-income people usually work till they drop dead or are useless, whichever comes first. I am not being hard-hearted; I am criticizing a society that still allows this to happen.)

Retirement almost always involves financial loss; few people have managed to accumulate enough money to keep on living in the style to which they became accustomed in their peak earning years. Even if they think they have enough when they start out down the sunset trail, fixed income pitted against rising living costs, financial disasters in their investment or annuity plans, and major unforeseen repairs to house or body can wreck their best-laid plans. It's worse if retirement takes place shortly after or shortly before the death of a spouse — particularly for women, I was going to say, but only in a financial sense. (The income of elderly single men is three thousand or four thousand dollars higher than that of elderly single women.) That wouldn't be fair, however. Elderly widowers, who have a greater tendency to remarry than do elderly widows, also die earlier and commit suicide in greater numbers.

Even alive and well, healthy and wealthy, who are these retired persons? Who are these people who have lost their role in life? Men take retirement worse than women, mostly because they have it worse. Their title changes; their venue changes, they're home all the time; their entire routine has been wiped out. The wife of a retiree, so the story goes, continues in the work she has been doing all her life, that is, home-making, with only this understanding conceded to her: that she married her husband for better or for worse, but now she has him for lunch — also elevenses, teatime, and underfoot — or as one English friend of mine put it, "on top of me all day." If the woman has worked all her life outside the home, then she has an adjustment to make as well, and a couple of new roles to play: stay-at-home housewife and the only person her husband has left to order around. The joke for the man is that he has joined the Honeydo Corporation ("Honey, do this; Honey, do that . . .").

Enforced unemployment is the worst "novel event," worse than retirement, because it threatens financial ruin, loss of status and shelter, and real hunger and physical suffering in addition to the loss of self-esteem one suffers when one cannot fend for oneself or provide for one's family. We seem to forget that retirement is also unemployment, especially enforced retirement. If we are achievement-oriented, and most people are in this century, then we want to do well whatever we do. Part of doing well is to acknowledge no loss either of ability or energy.

"Two weeks," says Alex Comfort in his book *A Good Age*, "is about the ideal length of time to retire." Then the retired person should get back to work, perhaps different work, perhaps unpaid work, but work nevertheless, a project that gives meaning and definition to free time, work that Comfort calls a "second trajectory." There is a good, tough optimism in this attitude and a pragmatic approach to retirement that may well be able to handle dwindling energy and money, but the role loss has not even been considered.

Retired people must go through the shock of change, adapting to a new lifestyle, the denial that they have changed, the anger that no one pays attention to them any more or even remembers their former value, the depression as they sink into a sense of worthlessness, and the despair at having lost their role in life. The grief involved is for the loss of any meaning in what they're doing.

At this point, what is known as "cramming for your exams" begins. Retired people are not really seeking a candle to light their way to dusty death, certainly not at first. They have miraculously — not merely — reached the stage of human development when they might be expected legitimately to search for meaning. If they use their grief at their loss creatively, they stand a fair chance of finding it. It's nicer if they have company.

The elderly bereaved don't have the same resilience or the energy to make a new life for themselves. Depending on the age at which they are bereaved, they don't have much time left themselves. It's not easy to find new mates or new friends at any age, but it's even more difficult when new ones are in short supply (another of the reasons why fewer older women remarry than do older men: there are more women than men extant). Old friends are dead. Sociologists commenting on the loneliness of the elderly usually find that they are bereaved as well, and depressed. "It's getting so," said one old woman, "I know more people in the cemetery than on the street."

Young widows and widowers are both fascinated and repelled by their new self-image: "I would find myself saying to myself, 'Why did this happen to me?' But there was also an element of fascination with the adventure — I mean, to be a widower at the age of twenty-nine?"

Most of them feel almost as if they're play-acting. Maybe they'll wake up and find it was a bad dream. This can't be real. The denial is very strong because their bereavement is out of sync with their age. Death and youth aren't supposed to go together, right? So, what are they doing posing in this picture edged in black?

Well, we all know by now that death is no respecter of age, or youth. It may not hang crepe on the doors any more, but it puts unappetizing labels on the bereaved and swathes their sexuality (among other things) with stereotyped images. Amazingly, women often find themselves at a loss for a label after all these years. So many women have said to me (more Universal Script?), "I used to be my father's daughter, my husband's wife, my children's mother, my boss's 'girl.' Suddenly I am me — whoever that is." It's exhilarating but also terrifying, depending on one's age and attitude, suddenly to find oneself without a self-image, with a new role to mold.

Parents who have lost a child often do not entirely lose the role of parent if they have other children. What they do lose is the image of themselves as caretakers and protectors of their young. Somehow, despite all their efforts, they lost one. Somehow, it must be their fault, some element that was missing in them — genetically, psychologically — that contributed to their child's death. They lose part of a shining image and acquire a sense of failure. I know mothers who lose an infant through miscarriage or stillbirth feel this particularly.

So our self-image keeps twisting and changing before our very eyes. Much as we would like it to stay put, to be stable and reassuring and admirable, it doesn't. When we lose, it loses. When we lose something or someone close to us, it loses its shine and its sheen. When it's really damaged, we hardly know ourselves. What, then, can we expect from others?

14. Loss of Neighborhood

There is no sorrow above
The loss of a native land.
— EURIPIDES

LIKE A GOLDFISH SWIMMING IN A BOWL OF WATER, WE ARE unaware of the element we move in until there's a crack in the bowl. Just as we take the earth's air and water for granted until they are threatened, so we assume the consistency and safety of our own milieu until it changes. There are still people who have never left the town they were born in, who have lived all their lives in one place and who will die there. They're getting rarer, though. Circumstances force a lot of people out of their birthplace before they can make a conscious choice: they move as children with their families or in with relatives or to foster homes after the death of one or both of their parents. Earthquakes, fire, flood, famine, and war drive others from their homes, while restlessness and ambition pull others out of orbit. Jobs and marriage move people to other places, and divorce and retirement can mean a change of place as well as lifestyle. Mobility is a given these days, upward or horizontal but frequent. When the moves are for happy, growing reasons, they may still be stressful, but the stress is not compounded by the heavy emotional burden that death or divorce lays on them.

People move so frequently that others don't give them much support or sympathy for the losses they suffer, even when the larger loss that caused the move was traumatic. Thus, in addition to the shock and anger and fear they may be suffering, they are now also losing roots and familiarity and faces, and no one seems to notice. They lose confidence and trust and they often lose their way. A number of women who have written to me were stranded by a move that took place just *before* the death of their husband, leaving them wondering how to make friends, and, most especially, how to help their children find their way. There's only so much reaching out (more like clutching) a newly bereaved, newly moved person can do. I hope that strangers will become friends, and help the alien bereaved over root shock.

Deracinated, it's called, deriving from the French *racine*, meaning "root." Gardeners talk about root shock for plants; it's worse for people. In some way, people who have left their roots are forever foreign. Rootless.

Confidence and trust in the place of one's roots are never completely guaranteed, of course. Confidence comes with a knowledge of the safe places, and trust rests on the expectations of predictable behavior in others. When a death or divorce or similar Life Event has caused the move, both confidence and trust are in short supply. One has a tendency to stumble and to lose one's way. People like to feel they can find their way, literally and figuratively.

Losing my way is one of the things I do best. I could even do it in my home town, but I have been doing it with dismaying and increasing frequency since I left it. It's a terrible thing to be a stranger in the streets. No longer a citizen of Home Town, one becomes a transient. No longer the efficient, self-confident, self-reliant person one thought one was, one has lost, along with that larger role (wife, husband, mate) the First Role, that of human being. The world isn't going by; I am.

The most thorough, thoughtful moving company in the world cannot ease a person into a new place as smoothly as it does the furniture. Welcome Wagons and Newcomers' Clubs can't dispel the feeling of strangeness. Local maps and a new library card don't do all that much for a sense of belonging. The tension of meeting new people all the time and of being constantly affable, even to people one doesn't particularly like, drains energy in someone whose supply of it is already depleted.

Even within the same city, a move presents losses. One loses one's familiar and cooperative neighbors. Visits by invitation never replace the daily, familiar, casual intercourse of neighborliness. Young children, especially, are affected by the loss of the neighboring playmates because they have lost control as well; they can't see each other without help from their elders. A move during a child's high-school years can constitute a devastating loss; there is no time left to replace the friendships of a (short) lifetime. If their move has been caused by a Life Event, that is, by a death or divorce, it becomes to them another example of the carpet having been pulled out from under them, through no fault of their own and without their having any say in the matter.

One would like to hope that the move is for the better but it often isn't. It's frequently forced by financial circumstances and usually means smaller, cheaper accommodation. It's accompanied by other losses not only of familiarity but also of basic security. Life will never be the same again.

Grieving for the comfortable safety of the former home (if indeed it was comfortable and safe) follows some of the stages of grief, if to a lesser degree, and with more speed. The most apparent is denial.

People are slow to accept some of the losses of a move and practice a kind of denial for some time. They still go back to their dentist in the other place, or hang onto their insurance agent, or return to a favorite restaurant whenever they're in the vicinity, and certainly go back to visit old friends. Oddly, most bereaved or divorced people discover that old friends are more welcoming when one is merely an occasional visitor than when one is a constant presence and an embarrassing reminder (reminder of mortality, reminder of one's indifference).

The very act of moving house is hard enough. I can still long for the luxury of former cupboard and closet space, or shed a nostalgic tear for the dream kitchen in an old house we renovated. Until I moved to the shores of a lake, I used to miss the backyard swimming pool we had in Stratford. When I have trouble finding something, I often remember exactly where it was in a former home. The dislocation of things is an outward symbol of the dislocation of our minds. As the old granny said, "Three moves is as good as a fire!" — and just as disrupting.

Adjustment may come more easily when the reason for a move is happy, or when the goal of the move is survival. No matter what the reason, the move itself still presents a shock to the system and to the mind. When it follows too closely on a major life change, it has a cumulative effect. Alvin Toffler warns of this in *Future Shock*. The trick is "not to suppress change, but to manage it."

As if one could suppress change. Things happen. But the management of change, how is it done? The birth — or the death — of a child should not be followed too quickly by a relocation; a job transfer should not follow on the heels of a divorce; a recent widow shouldn't *think* of moving for at least a year after the death of her husband, nor a widower of remarriage.

We have commented on the effect of too many Life Events packed into too short a space of time. A move presents so many changes in lifestyle adjustments, the breaking of familiar habits and routines, that, taken at the wrong time, it can compound the problems surrounding other losses. Everyone needs a sense of continuity, a feeling of stability, some reassurance that life is not completely without meaning. What we need is a little light on the subject. So we stamp our feet and yell, "I *know* I have lightbulbs. I just don't know where they are."

We all have some inner construct of reality that enables us to make it through the day. If people's sense of reality is too much changed, too much challenged, then their ability to cope is damaged and they will show reactions similar to grief: (root) shock, denial (I still use my second-last city's general insurance agent), searching (for those lightbulbs), depression (yearning for the kitchen cupboards) and, finally, acceptance.

> Once we had a beautiful cottage by a lake
> But it burned down.
> It's still there in my memory, bigger now than it was,
> And the weather is always perfect
> And the tree-toad sings all night on the door
> And ice-worms gleam in the black water
> Still as glass.

> Once we had a beautiful kitchen in a house
> But we sold it and moved away.
> It's still there in my memory, neater now than it was,
> And the shelves are always tidy
> And the ovens are full of cookies and meat
> And the floor gleams with a waxy shine
> Like an ad.

Once we had a beautiful marriage in a life
But you died and it was over.
You're still there in my memory, handsomer than you were,
And our health is always excellent
And we are never tired or cranky
And your body covers mine with a perfect love
And it's all true.

15. Parenting After Loss

I think every parent must have a sense of failure, even of sin, merely in remaining alive after the death of a child. One feels that it is not right to live when one's child has died, that one should somehow have found the way to give one's life to save his life.
— FRANCES GUNTHER

WHEN A CHILD DIES, A PARENT LOSES NOT ONLY THE CHILD but the image of oneself as the protector. Obviously a failure as a caregiver, else the child would still be alive, the bereaved parent (whether or not there are other children) has suffered a damaging loss of self. The role has been taken away or, if not removed, then challenged. Much the same thing happens when a parent loses total or partial custody of a child or children through divorce. The image of oneself as competent caregiver, possible role model, mentor, and power source is severely damaged.

Other losses occur as well, not as drastic as death or divorce, but ones that bring a sense of diminishment. Every gain, we know, is accompanied by a loss. Whose gain? Whose loss? When a mother weans her baby, she loses the infant's sweet dependence on her for nourishment and life itself. The first day of school marks a step away from the home and toward independence. Going away to camp, learning to drive, leaving for college, moving out of the home, setting up independent housekeeping—all these moves toward adulthood, gains for the child, represent losses to the parents. Parents wouldn't have it any other way; the steps toward independence are natural and inevitable. If the steps are arrested, for reasons of a child's handicap—emotional, mental, or physical — the curtailment causes more pain. We suffer our children's losses as well as our own.

Brave little person, trudging off to school, flying off to adventure, at whatever age. Most parents wish they could fight all their children's battles for them and shield them from all pain. Being wrapped in cotton batting never did anyone any good, though. Overprotection stunts growth, hinders development, and saps strength. The only way to keep one's children, parents learn early on, is to let them go. Hovering parents and smothering love force them away much sooner than they might otherwise have gone.

It's even harder to be this tough when a child has already died, or had an accident, or been killed. Any death diminishes one's trust in life. The death of a child breaks not only trust but faith. If it was so easy for one to die, why not two? (It happens.) Letting a child out of one's sight becomes an act of faith, and of great courage. One has to learn to let go.

The phrase "Empty Nest Syndrome" was coined to describe the uselessness that parent birds — particularly, think the psychologists, the mother — feel when their children fly away. I don't think such parents feel all that abandoned. Perhaps an earlier generation, old at forty, dead at sixty-five, felt life was closing in by the time the children were on their own. Their task was finished, there was nothing of importance left to do. When all the meaning of life is invested in the next generation, this attitude of emptiness might be understandable. As it is now, children are grown up and leave while their parents still have a lot of living left to do themselves. Women not only survive childbirth but stay younger longer and live more years than they ever have. Even the menfolk have a longer life expectancy than they've ever had. So there is no reason that the exodus of the children should mark the end of parents' lives. There's lots to look forward to: travel and time together (if they're lucky), and second-trajectory careers.

Not only that, the Empty Nest Syndrome is an inaccurate description of what really happens. I call it the "Revolving Nest Syndrome": no matter which way one turns, the kids are still around. Adult children keep coming back. Prolonged education, split marriages, and financial setbacks are among the many events that drive children back to the parental nest. Many parents are dismayed at this homing-pigeon instinct in their children and wish they would leave, once and for all. They're welcome for Sunday dinners or Thanksgiving weekends, but enough is enough. This reluctance on the part of adult children to cut the cord can threaten parents more than the kids' eagerness to leave. Parents lose their privacy and well-earned rest, as well as some easing of the financial burden and the freedom to explore the rest of their lives without interruption. To everything there is a season, and the Golden Years, we think, were not meant to be tarnished with faded hopes and continuing dark responsibilities.

Aging parents face the possibility of a different, sharper loss, that of their own dwindling strength, both physical and financial or — worse — of their incompetence, a dismaying inability to look after themselves, and the disappearance of self. When children have to become parents to their parents, both parties perceive the necessity as against nature, and it hurts all concerned. As people survive other diseases and live longer, more of them will encounter this baffling and painful loss in themselves and their loved ones.

A daughter reports standing at the checkout counter, putting back the things her mother keeps taking out of the display rack. Her parent smiles at her; it has become a game. The parenting child smiles back.

"Mama, you are a scamp."

"I know."

"I love you, Mama."

"I love you too."

Love does not explain grief, nor does it make it less painful, but sometimes it helps.

16. Loss of Youth, Innocence, Sexuality

Your body does not bear thinking about
but I think about it

Your mouth is full of clay
and mine still longs for yours

THE SEXUAL GRIEVING PROCESS REQUIRES ENORMOUS AND equal amounts of heroism and humor, especially, I want to say, in the younger bereaved, but that is selfish and narrow-minded of me. I was forty-two when I was widowed, and I would not wish on anyone the experience of being a widow in one's forties. I used to pray for the sap to stop running. However, for an older widow the empty space in the bed after twice as many years as I had must seem like a black hole.

As for widowers, it's harder for men because their sexuality is, for most of them, their only means of getting in touch with themselves. The world out there is to conquer — or at least not to be defeated by. The world in here is to *love* — or at least to be comforted by. "To want too little from the love object is as self-defeating as to want too much," says Ernest Becker in *The Denial of Death*. Men who find substitutes too quickly want too little, but they want it right away.

Women "go foolish" (rhymes with *bullish*). That's an expression I picked up in Bermuda when I was writing my book about widowhood. Tell women not to go foolish, I was told, and I did tell them. Later, back in Bermuda, I mentioned the expression to a cab driver (he corrected my pronunciation) and he laughed and laughed. Apparently, it's a well-known behavior pattern. So I mentioned it again in my book for singles.

Do not, I ordered primly, go foolish. But I did. I didn't realize it at the time; I thought I was behaving rationally and with great circumspection. But I went very foolish. Not by way of defense or absolution, I want to say that women do — go foolish, that is. I'm not sure they can avoid it. It's part of the grieving process — and one of the most difficult parts because there is so much silence surrounding it, and so much shame and guilt. I'll deal with the stages of guilt on the sexual level only, and fast-frame. These apply to men as well, but women seem to be more foolish — and vulnerable?

Shock: whether the death of a loved one has been anticipated or not, the female body goes into a deep-freeze. I have read accounts by widowers describing their sexual madness in the first year of bereavement. In all fairness, I think the dividing line is not according to gender but to age. Older widowers tend to behave more like widows of all ages; they are numb. One widower described being approached by a prostitute. "I can't even make a fist," he told her.

Limp, in limbo, barely functioning physically as a human being — of course, if one can't eat or sleep, why should one be expected to be sexually inclined? Yet widows are rapidly approached by men offering solace. If solace were all! During the shock phase, sex is the last thing on the mind of the bereaved. Comfort and hugs, yes, but no genital nuzzling. Unfortunately, warm bodies without strings (and knobs and hard things) are hard to come by — for a long time.

During the denial phase, stray streamers of sex may shoot out, but more likely from the eyes than from the loins of the survivor. In the disbelief and rejection of what has happened, the bereaved may clutch at other bodies (more likely pillows) for comfort. Again, it has been my observation that this happens more with men, but it may be, too, that men have more opportunity, and are more accustomed to making the first move — and to being accepted. There are female sexual social work-ers, too, women who offer the comfort without strings that widowers need. I suppose they are the female counterpart of the men I have mentioned who offer comfort to widows. Men in this situation still tend to make the first move, whether or not the woman has indicated any willingness. Women of a certain age (divorcées as well as widows), and I include my then forty-two-year-old self among them, find lust without love bewildering. They tend to misinterpret the offer of the body advanced so freely; they think it is theirs to keep. They continue to make this mistake.

The anger that follows denial is physically painful. When my sexual needs began to rise, I tried self-pleasuring but it didn't work. I ended up racked in sobs rather than orgasm, screaming in pain and anger, shouting my rage at my husband for leaving me like this, so thwarted, so yearning, helpless, and frustrated and empty. I suppose for men who are looking for it, they can see the electrical charges sparking from a woman's body when she reaches this stage. If someone moves on her then, he has a fair chance of succeeding. And then something worse happens: shame, guilt, horror.

When a woman goes to bed with someone after her mate has died, she feels as if she has committed adultery. She has been unfaithful, and here's the cruncher: not just to his memory but to his *body*. In fact, eerily enough, his body is there in bed with her and her lover — three of them! Not kinky at all, but disturbing and sad, overwhelmingly sad. Other widows told me of this experience before I encountered it myself.

The sadness for the woman is a low not to be believed, or desired. Most women my age are like me — like I was: one man away from virginity. Those who are younger feel cheated; they thought they had more years of togetherness coming to them. All of us feel incredibly naive, even adolescent. Not only ashamed and furtive but eager and embarrassed, a widow in her forties and fifties feels like a superannuated teenager, a teenager coping with her first dates, but perhaps less confident than she was then, and certainly more scared.

There's more to be scared of these days. Back in the sixties, during the sexual revolution, the Pill took care of everything (except one's self-respect). The Pill is useless to a woman in her forties, with a higher risk of heart attack or stroke. Even if she has her tubes tied to free herself from an unwanted pregnancy, she isn't safe, not these days. Sexually transmitted diseases pose a threat to anyone contemplating carefree sex. As the ads on TV tell us, a casual affair doesn't involve only two people; it involves the partners each of them has had for the previous eight to ten years. That's not the kind of statement that inspires a great deal of confidence in anyone entering the meat market after a hiatus of some twenty or thirty years. A woman will experience not only fear but anger.

The anger is expressed now not only at Fate and her husband but also at herself. How can I be like this? What do I think I'm doing? I must be out of my mind. (She has, in fact, gone foolish.) She withdraws, she closes tighter than ever, she takes to long walks, or swimming, or tennis, some physical activity to work off her sexual tension (it helps). Ironically, she also starts looking better, and she knows it.

I must say, the morning after experiencing my first pass (thorough but incomplete; it took a while to break the barriers) since Bill had died, I was, needless to say, preoccupied with it. I had never considered myself particularly good-looking (what has that got to do with it?), and my husband used to argue with me about that; he kept asking me why I would never believe him. "When are you going to believe me?" he would say with some exasperation.

I had an errand to run that particular morning after (the pass) and, as I got into the car, I heard Bill's voice as clearly as I've ever heard anyone's voice, say to me, "*Now* do you believe me?" I laughed out loud. It was the first time I had laughed, really laughed, at myself since Bill's death — *two years* earlier. It was a full year after that before I finally went to bed with the person who made the pass (he was nothing if not persistent), and then it almost killed me.

Statistics exist on just about any topic worth running a questionnaire on; stats tell me that it takes widows longer than divorcées to go to bed with a new man after the Life Event that changed their lives and upheaved their sexuality. My fall into bed hit just about right on average, although other widows I spoke to were running a little ahead of me. The ones who did were younger than I was; the ones who didn't do anything were considerably older.

According to experts, a woman is supposed to reach her sexual peak in her forties (a man reaches his considerably younger — another reason to consider older woman/younger man relationships!). How very frustrating for her, then, if her life circumstances force her to spend these years alone — or going foolish. Perhaps this accounts for the next phase of her sexual grieving: the *searching*.

Searching or yearning doesn't always play a great part in the stages of grief. I have indicated its usual manifestations. In terms of sexual grieving it figures largely. I'm still not sure if I can define or describe the search. I don't think it's for a new mate, at least, I discovered in retrospect that, in my case, it wasn't. As I have said, I found that I ran from eligible, possible liaisons, somehow preferring someone more remote, geographically distant and unavailable, so as not to threaten my equilibrium or new-found self. Even in the midst of all the searching for Other, widows are terrified of losing Self. The ones I know who have remarried never asked the questions I was asking about who they were and where they were going. They had too much invested in their lives already to start asking those questions this far along.

I wasn't clear about all this. Few people are, in the midst of new experiences. It's only with hindsight that I see more clearly what was going on, what I was doing. I know now that my search was not for a substitute. I also know that I was very self-indulgent (not extremely; I turned down far more opportunities than I accepted). One thing I learned — no, two things — that I wish all young women could learn. One is the value of lust; the other is the distinction between uncertainty and love. Why does one learn these things only through grief? Because grieving is a creative, learning process, that's why.

Many younger women confuse lust with love, more frequently in my era and earlier, but perhaps again now as the fear of sexually transmitted diseases has imposed some of the same restraints on premarital sex that the threat of shotgun marriages, abortion butchery, and expulsion from society did for women in earlier times. In his book *Marriage and Morals*, first published in 1927, Bertrand Russell commented on this confusion a young woman feels (used to feel?) when she first encounters sex and mistakes physical passion for lasting love.

The search goes on: the mass media are still selling the idea that "some day my prince will come." In the case of the bereaved, the searching also goes on, accompanied all the while by depression. Those "now" beads I have mentioned are never added to so ecstatically or fingered so morosely as during the roller-coaster ride of bereaved sex. Men — widowers — suffer this too; I know they are not exempt. I have talked to lots of widowers, corresponded with more, and read articulate accounts by others, so I am well aware of their trauma. No one can claim a corner on pain, and I will not claim it in the name of widows. Depression is genderless.

Also devastating. Sexual depression is a monster because it combines self-accusation with self-pity, set within a shameless shameful hunger like a serpent crawling through one's body.

I realize some people will be repelled by this, but I declare openly that masturbation is a useful tool in the grieving process and, ultimately, of course, in the discovery of self. Some people don't need it, never will. Perhaps they're lucky. Maybe some people never had a problem. They're lucky too. Others are as reticent and embarrassed as I was, and they may find themselves more comfortable in themselves and, incidentally, less in danger of going foolish.

Acceptance on the sexual level of grieving implies many things: acceptance of one's bed, empty or not, acceptance of one's body, acceptance of the full range of human experience rarely explored by those whose lives have not been transformed by death. When I was fearful and ashamed and holding back from reaching for what I needed (at the time), I came across this phrase that helped me. It describes someone who has to make a decision to let go and take risks because he has "a tool too keen for timid safety."

We all have that tool — our mind — if we dare hone it and test it. I used that phrase as a challenge to myself, at once my gauntlet and my guerdon, as I rode out to tilt at my sexual windmills, "with a tool too keen for timid safety." Acceptance, then, finally, means a confidence in one's tools and skills, those of the body as well as of the mind. No need for timid safety when one has traversed this last field, and survived.

One need not have suffered the loss of a sexual partner through death to go through the grieving process in all its steps. It can come with the first promise of one's own death — the inevitable aging process — and it can come after divorce. The same old stages are applicable: shock, denial, anger, depression, bargaining, and oh-so-reluctant acceptance. The shock with aging does not come with one sudden blow; it drops like acid, slow and erosive. There is no one day that anyone says, "Today I am old." When the first gray hair appears, it is sharply plucked out. The first wrinkle is more like a slight smudge, more easily erased than the furrow/trough/rut it will grow into. The first failure of the body to respond to one's needs — the extra stretch required, the extra spurt of speed, the extra lift of strength, the extra mile that just isn't forthcoming — is easily (at first) attributed to a late night, a hard week, a temporary lapse.

A deeper depression sets in with the mid-life crisis. Different events bring it on in different lives. For a man the first hint of it might come when his son beats him at tennis—or chess? For another man, it might come when the new young woman in the typing pool ignores his gallantries or calls him sir. Or it may come the first time he prefers to make love in the morning rather than the night before, when he was too tired but blamed it on booze or the hour. Physical signs of aging like receding hairlines and love handles bother men, but the real crisis comes through their work as they realize they've gone as far as they're going to go, that this is as good as it's going to be. Aspirations deflate, and they must reconcile themselves to mediocrity. (This happens to women, too.) Sometimes they blame others for their aging and lack of opportunity: the breaks, the boss, the wife.

The easiest one to do something about is the wife. He gets his hair cut, has it blow-dried, and trades in the old lady for a newer model. A young wife, and often a new family, give the illusion of youth, a second start, anyway, and wipe away depression for a while. What this kind of divorce does to the first wife is devastating and depressing in the extreme. I know women to whom this has happened who have never learned how to sleep again, years after the rejection.

Thus many older women suffer from men's grief over their lost youth as well as from their own. Just when they're feeling most vulnerable, they get dumped. About two-thirds of unmarried women now are divorced, a reversal from sixty years ago when two-thirds of them were widowed. Married, or un-, women grieve over their lost youth more than do men because they lose more. Aging inflicts vicious penalties on women, more uncharitable than those imposed on men. There is a double standard of aging far harsher than the double standard of sexual behavior.

After the acid shocks and the holding actions of denial, and the bargaining, which goes hand in glove with denial, a deep rage grows in most women—not depression, not anger, but *rage*. No one likes to be ignored; to be invisible is worse. Some men (in books) theorize that the invisibility of women of a certain age has to do with their uselessness. Once they're past the child-bearing age, they are useless to men, therefore irrelevant, therefore invisible. So men, it is implied, respond to younger women, that is, women of child-bearing age, only because they are so aware of their responsibility to the species. Their aim in sex is apparently procreation, solely. Hah. The youth and beauty of the rose attracts the bee only that nature may be served. The old rose can get lost in a pot-

153

pourri for all the bee cares. The bee has propagation on his mind, the perpetuation of life. Selfless bee!

In his book *The Denial of Death*, Ernest Becker has a few annoying things to say about women and menopause. In an argument that considers only men's denial of death and ignores women's reaction, Becker buys Freud's notion that females think they've been castrated when they first discover males have penises and they don't. Becker thinks that women regard menopause as a repetition of their castration experience. "It will be easy for us to understand," he writes (us being men), "that menopause simply reawakens the horror of the body, the utter bankruptcy of the body. . . . Menopause is a sort of 'animal birthday' that specifically marks the physical career of degeneration." The end is in sight, he says, "the absolute determinism of death." Since men don't have such an 'animal birthday,' Becker reasons, they don't have to face this fact of life. Woman is less fortunate, he thinks, because "death doesn't keep knocking at her door only to be ignored (as men ignore their aging) but kicks it in to show himself full in the face."

- "Dollink," goes the Miami joke, "have you hit the menopause yet?" "I haven't even hit the Fontainebleau," is the reply.
- "I don't mind having a grandchild," says the new grandfather. "I just hate the thought of sleeping with a grandmother."
- "I get so tired of the speckled hand being laid sympathetically on mine," says one arrogant old widower.

Menopause is nothing to a woman compared to men's treatment of it and her, and of her aging. Granted, there are physical symptoms that some women suffer from to greater or lesser extent, but most women agree with Margaret Mead, the anthropologist who had so much to say to North American women, when she predicted that women would enjoy their most productive years *after the menopause*. Menopause is not a cause of women's grieving, but male attitudes to it are, hence the rage.

Aging, for men and women, should provide the opportunity for self-mourning. It's the beginning of the countdown, and while the countdown may be blessedly slow (and healthy!), we know it is ultimately inexorable. We must begin, as Martin Luther once said, "to taste death as though it were present," not in a morbid way, but with gratitude and serenity.

The aged are serene (if they're wise). They have lived long enough to see many die before them, loved and young, suffering or suddenly. It doesn't hurt as much to say goodbye, possibly because one hasn't long before one also leaves. The very fact that one has survived so much in the past offers reassurance that one can bear more, one's own death as well as that of others. "Old age is not so bad," said Maurice Chevalier, "when you consider the alternative."

VI

DEATH OF A RELATIONSHIP

There are other kinds of death, as devastating and far-reaching as the physical demise of a loved one.

17. Divorce and Separation

Divorce is having all your teeth out one by one.
— JANE BAILEY-BLOOD STRETE

SOME EXPERTS NOW SAY THAT THE SOCIAL READJUSTMENT Rating Scale points for bereavement and divorce should be reversed, giving the highest stress rating of 100 to divorce and 73 to the death of a mate. There is something to be said for this. Because both parties are still alive, divorce can go on inflicting sharp slaps of pain every time one of them gets vindictive again, whereas, with death, one of the parties has stopped talking back. This next line has been said so often to me it's almost as if it came from the Universal Script, except it's said by divorced people: "At least you know where your husband is."

In spite of the fact that one in four or five marriages ends in divorce now, society is still judgmental about it. Recently divorced people wonder bitterly who got custody of their friends. Some friends get so nervous about playing favorites that they do nothing at all until it's too late. Then both parties assume the choice has been made and never see each other again — another loss. One divorced man told me he felt as if he had leprosy. One divorced woman commented that "people fade away as if I were invisible." It's not paranoia, not just their imagination. Former friends can be quite judgmental and choose the spouse who strikes them as being the most hurt, the most moral, the most vulnerable, or the most useful. It depends on the friends, I guess.

Society creates a hostile environment for the bereaved, providing no breathing space and little freedom to mourn or to grieve. At least with death there is some small, accepted ritual in the first immediate days surrounding the funeral. No one sends a casserole to celebrate a divorce. Or flowers for a decree nisi. As one divorced woman said, "I've lost my husband, my house, my friends, my status, but I'm not supposed to let it get me down. Chin up!" But, a divorced man said, "Why should I support my children? I never get to see them. I'm painted as a monster. I don't know them any more."

Divorced people don't seem to know their friends any more either. Some of the shafts of anger flying around are aimed at the friends as well as at the ex. For this and other reasons, any encounter with a recently divorced person can be quite volatile, not to say distressing. Separation, called "the poor person's divorce," can also be damaging to friendships. In this case, the friends really don't know which way to turn, or what to say. If the couple gets back together, both will resent what was said as well-intentioned advice if it maligned one or the other of them. Because of this wariness on the part of friends, separated couples can feel very isolated — yet another loss.

The people who get left in divorce claim all the pain as their own, but the people who do the leaving say it hurts them too. Guilt versus rejection. Either feeling gives one a not-very-pleasant self-image. "Dumper or dumpee," says one divorcee, "you leave your *esteem* behind." As for the self that was invested in the sum of both their parts, it must be withdrawn, propped up, made to move under its own volition again. The relationship guru of the 1970s, Merle Shain, said, "It's awful to be rejected but there is pain in rejecting too and not having your needs met is no worse than meeting those of others out of guilt or fear instead of love." At one stage, sorting out and identifying the emotions becomes a task in itself.

Divorce is particularly damaging because there's a hook on the end of the knife. First, there is the shock of the death of love and then there is the shock of a new life without it. A curious relief follows the physical parting. After what may have been months or even years of ugly fights and bitter recriminations, or at best an uneasy hostile truce, the silence and relative peace after the storm offer a curious alleviation of the emotions.

Withdrawal symptoms play their part in the pain A.D. (After Divorce). A physical departure has taken place. Just as the emotions are in danger of being buried with the deceased, so they tend to leave with the departed even though he or she is still on this earth. As the rage subsides, it leaves an empty space achingly similar in its dimensions to the hole left in one's life by a death. The anger destroys the past. At least with bereavement the past stays where it is and can be cherished. A bitter divorce colors the past ugly too. The amnesia caused by anger threatens one's identity. "I'm nothing now," a newly divorced woman said to me. "I'm a blank."

Fear quickly rushes in to fill the empty space. The familiar questions rise up like specters: Who am I? Where am I going now? The mind starts playing tricks then as ambivalence waffles in. Maybe it wasn't so bad. Perhaps it would help to give it another shot. At least there was company; everyone knows misery loves company. In the flickering light of doubt, grapefruit for one doesn't look as attractive as the crashing dinner plates and a live body banging and shouting at the other side of the table or bed. If the person left has the children, then she (usually she) can't afford grapefruit. She's trying to take care of the whole family, minus one, with a fraction of the former income. She's lucky if the support payments arrive on time (75 to 90 percent of court-ordered support payments are defaulted on). Current statistics reveal that a man's income goes up by 73 percent following divorce, whereas a woman's goes down by 42 percent. And yet a current joke goes like this:

Man: What do you want? Anything!

Woman: A divorce.

Man: I hadn't planned on spending that much.

One does hear of amicable divorces. I know of a couple of reluctantly cooperative ones, but of only one where the ex-wife and remarried husband are really good friends and she is a welcome guest in the bemused second wife's home. I heard of one marriage that broke up when the husband came out of the closet and moved in with a long-term lover. The new male couple became the ex-wife's staunchest supporters. When life got too hectic for her, raising her kids and her second husband's kids, she would go and spend a weekend with her former mate and his lover. They would pamper her and give her TLC and wine by the fire and breakfast in bed and send her back to her beloved family as rejuvenated as if she had been at a spa. Her whole family mourned with his lover at the funeral of her first husband, who died of AIDS.

Several divorced couples, one or both halves of which have remarried, still go to bed with each other now and then, so I guess that's pretty friendly. I must comment that when the ex-husband has remarried and the first wife has not, such behavior seems to me more like exploitation, as if the man is developing a small harem, but I'm just giving the news here. Perhaps it's reassuring to know that most divorced couples are predictably bitter and force their friends to make choices and take sides.

Recently divorced men and women are dangerous; they tend to go as foolish as Bermuda widows and they have trouble remembering names. A feeling of rejection drives them into brief liaisons (called one-night stands) in an attempt to reassure themselves that they are still attractive to the opposite sex. Sometimes, too, an unacknowledged desire for revenge makes them treat their short-lived loves with something less than honesty or tenderness. They often hint to their exes of their nocturnal activity in the hope that it will hurt them. None of this behavior is admirable but one hopes for the sake of their health that these wounded people are more circumspect, that is, careful, than they were in the 1960s and 1970s because they are considerably more at risk. Sex is not safe without a safe — rubber, parachute, condom — in designer colors now. Both men and women have to be very careful. Sexual grieving is a precarious business and could be damaging to one's health.

As with death, children are the neglected grievers in divorce. More than anyone, they have divided loyalties; they fear being forced to make a choice. If the settlement has caused a move, they have lost not only their secure family home but their accustomed environment and friends. If their mother gets custody (and most women do, unless the father contests), they also face a sickening drop in lifestyle and a restricted future with less opportunity for a good education and a good career. Add to that the emotional fear: if their parents' love for each other has stopped, may it not also stop for them?

For many women, the grieving after a divorce translates as guilt. Taking the blame for a husband who walked out on her, a woman I know said to me, "I feel like a failure. Where did I go wrong? What should I have done?" Society, too, often gives a woman the same feeling, that "if she'd satisfied her husband, he would have stayed home." This last is from a judge's statement as he handed out the settlement. Another judge said, "You women are liberated now, so take the consequences."

"In a divorce situation," sighed one weary divorcée, "life is one long negotiation." Here's a grim line from the Universal Script about divorce: "Divorce is a no-win situation." And yet a lot of people survive divorce these days. Somehow they struggle through the shock, denial, anger, and depression and come out on the other side.

I haven't mentioned depression yet, have I? Depression thumps along at the heels of anger, dragged in on an excess of emotion. Slowly, paralysis sets in. Everything is too much effort, and the world is bleak and colorless. Now is the time to beware of drugs — both over-the-counter and the harder stuff — as well as alcohol. Excesses of any kind appeal to the depressed because they help to mask painful feelings and push back consciousness — for a while. Not so incidentally, the drug-induced withdrawal of the remaining parent can be the final blow to children staggering from the impact of a divorce (or death) in the family. They may never be capable of real attachment again. There are just too many risks.

The bargaining stage of grief doesn't work too well in the case of divorce. Acceptance comes a lot later. Renegotiation, the management of change, must take place for those grieving over divorce to come to any successful conclusion. The divorced, like the bereaved, must learn to let go, to stop clutching at straws or scratching at faces, to learn to relax. Not easy. It may be hard to remember, but everyone should try, that the adversary, this monster one used to live with, is a human being, very human, all too human, not a fire-eating, sleep-destroying monster, just human, like oneself.

When people go into the pain, they can begin to understand themselves better. They see the reasons for the fights and betrayals and withdrawals, they see the weaknesses that cause them. When understanding comes, that's the beginning of forgiveness. Forgiveness is necessary for this grieving process to work its healing. To understand is to forgive — not without conflict, but this time the conflict is within oneself; not without some hardening of the arteries — no, stiffening of the spine. This is not to say that forgiveness means taking less of a settlement than one needs or deserves, nor does it mean letting the other person ignore or default the terms of the settlement. Forgiveness does not mean continuing to be beaten or abused and doing nothing about it; forgiveness does not mean sacrificing one's own integrity or beliefs for the sake of peace in our time. Forgiveness means staying open to reasonable negotiation while recognizing the incapacity of the other person to change.

"It would take a miracle": that's another line from the Universal Script.

Separated couples need a miracle, too, and some of them get it. Some of them make it back into a marriage, different people (different marriage!) than they were. For the time out, they go through many of the stages of grief that the divorced and bereaved suffer. For a time they are the living embodiment of another line from the Universal Script: "can't live with each other, can't live without each other." The lucky ones manage to live together again.

In *Creative Divorce*, the author, Mel Krantzler, tries to make a case for change and growth from this painful event. Again, it boils down to a discovery and a recovery of self. It's too bad such a recovery has to be so hard-won with so much human trial and error, and pain. It also requires time, patience, and communication. One must keep the lines open to keep on learning. If only there weren't so much to learn. Grieving — about one thing or another — is a lifetime occupation.

There are rewards. I know an older divorcée who had trouble finding enough work to keep her solvent who put her considerable skills at the service of a Third World country where she is teaching in a university and having the adventure of her life. I interviewed a young divorcée (whose husband married her next-door neighbor) who took a real-estate course and ended up making more money than her ex, and agreed that he need not pay her support any more. (He took her to court, however, to demand the return of his alimony plus interest because the dollar wasn't worth as much as when he started paying her.) She not only discovered herself, she found out exactly whom she had married all those years ago when she didn't know any better.

More often, however, the rewards are dubious and the pain uppermost. For example, I talked to a widower whose marriage to a younger woman lasted a year and a half and who had to split his life earnings and savings with her under a new family-law act. He may not have been entirely clear who he was, but he used to be rich. Not all the horror stories feature male villains.

I met a middle-aged man who went to pieces after his divorce (his fault, he says), who doesn't see his sons very often, and who is paying support for a baby boy a casual lover says is his. He is broke and alone and wondering what happened to his dream of the good life, and who is he, anyway, and where in hell is he going?

And so the grief of divorce goes on . . .

If my stories seem strange or odd that's because people do strange or odd things. Divorce means the death of a relationship and the same loss of control over one's life that happens with bereavement. A person goes missing from our lives, and we have to withdraw our emotional investment — the anger as well as the love. We have also lost some of the pain of the relationship and we gain an opportunity to change our lives and our selves. (Every loss is accompanied by a gain.) As with futile anger, change is best managed by changing our expectations.

"What I have learned," says one divorcée, "is not that others have changed so much or grown away from me, but that *I* have changed." The situation will never be as it was before; it's past, both the good and the bad parts. We must accept life for what it is now (thereby changing ourselves), and go on from there. If we can manage it with some grace and a little humor, so much the better.

"One of the fringe benefits of being handed back your life," said Merle Shain, "is being awarded custody of yourself." It costs a lot.

18. Family Changes After Loss

Maybe no one knows what is happening. However, one thing is often clear to an outsider: there is concerted family resistance to discovering what is going on, and there are complicated stratagems to keep everyone in the dark, and in the dark that they are in the dark.
— R.D. LAING

RIPPLES IN A POND. THE DOMINO EFFECT. EVERY CHANGE that occurs causes another change, a series of changes, and we are all affected. The changes within a family can shift the entire balance of power, destroy its equilibrium, tear its very fabric. No one is immune. No one can emerge unscathed from a major loss within the group. As if it were genetically encoded, the mutation starts early, and never stops.

John Bowlby, in his searching observation of separation and loss, destroyed the illusion that grief in childhood is short-lived, or that its responses are not like those of bereaved adults. On the contrary, at any age the yearning and searching for the lost loved one can go on for a lifetime. Bowlby quotes Freud writing to a friend who had lost a son.

> *Although we know that after such a loss the acute state of mourning will subside, we also know we shall remain inconsolable and will never find a substitute. No matter what may fill the gap, even if it be filled completely, it nevertheless remains something else. And actually* this is how it should be. *It is the only way of perpetuating that love which we do not want to relinquish* (Emphasis mine).

Bowlby emphasizes the need for a redefinition of both self and situation. Self we have considered; the need to recover one's investment of self, the necessity of coming to terms with a new definition of self, that is, no longer anyone's spouse or child or parent. Situation must also be reassessed: relinquishing hope for the recovery of the lost person, recognizing that the old situation can never be reestablished, in other words, changing one's expectations. Nowhere does this necessity apply more directly than to the immediate family. Nowhere do so many changes take place as in the family during or following a loss.

I have already considered some of the practical pressures of a terminal illness and what it does to family life and routine, and some of the side-effects of a bad financial situation in a divorce settlement and what that does to the lifestyle and future hopes of the family. Apart from these external stresses, there are internal changes. For example, a family may need a scapegoat, someone to act out the unexpressed anger of all the members, sometimes to take the place of the scapegoat who left or died. The chief service that the scapegoat provides is someone to blame. The thinking goes, "If I can blame someone else, then I'm not the one to blame."

And so we see a kid suddenly go off the rails after a death (frequently a suicide) or divorce in the family, defiant, seemingly unreachable, hitting sex or alcohol or drugs, and providing everyone with a legitimate source of anxiety and anger. Somehow the bad conduct is necessary to all the members of the family. They can be taken in by the act, including the scapegoat. On the other hand, if the scapegoat was the one to go, then maybe the ranks shift and the "good one" gets blamed for not helping or caring enough.

All of us engage in trade-offs all the time. People trade physical safety for emotional security, choosing to stay, for example, in a war-torn zone or a flood or earthquake area in order to be near a loved one. We often trade financial stability for emotional satisfaction (it's called marrying for love), but some people do the opposite, choosing money over affection. Whatever security means to us, that's what we choose; it always seems to involve a trade. (No one, it seems, can have everything, not all at once, not all of the time, not for long.) We all need security in whatever form it takes for us. Social workers have discovered the need for caution and deliberation before they recommend the removal of a child from an abusive home. That home still provides security—a terrible, hazardous kind of security—but, nevertheless, intense involvement. Grief at loss isn't caused by lost love alone, though love was usually present; grief springs from intense *involvement*. That's one of the reasons a widow emerging from a bad marriage can suffer more than one secure in the knowledge of her late husband's love. That's why the bereaved even welcome the pain because it means they are still alive. "I know I'm alive," says one widow, "because I still hurt."

When I was first widowed, I thought of the physical separation of war. My mother, like most of the North American women of her generation, was separated from my father for a number of years, in her case four years, two of them without contact other than letters when he was overseas. Many children didn't meet their fathers until they were four or five years old because they were conceived on the last leave before overseas service. As the time stretched out following Bill's departure from planet Earth, I compared the months and years slipping away to that separation — and anxiety — that other women who waited for husbands to return after a long absence have experienced. As I changed and grew over the first four years of my widowhood, I wondered more about those women. The adjustment period for those whose husbands returned from war must have been fraught. For the men, too. They had to change their occupations when they returned, in addition to resuming or beginning life with a stranger.

Following a death in their midst, family members go through similar psychological alterations. All are spotlighted by the harsh light self-conscious grief has focused on them. Grief is mightily self-conscious, as we know; that's how the self must be consciously withdrawn and readjusted.

"On your way up the ladder of life," goes a saying in my childhood autograph book, "may you never meet a friend going down." Yes, and vice versa. Financial setbacks, of course, trigger enormous changes within a family. In my mother's day, middle-class wives who lived through the Depression learned to make one dollar do the work of two and look like five. Keeping up appearances was as important as eating well. A man's home was his castle, and though the tapestries on the castle walls might be threadbare and the fire burned low, the drawbridge still worked and shut out the world. The lady of the house preserved the flame and his pride. We read horror stories of the Depression now, scarcely believing the pride that made a man starve his family and himself before accepting any social assistance (what little there was).

During a long, severe illness, including a terminal one, the balance of power shifts dramatically within a family. The sick one, child or adult, dominates the household. The changes to all concerned, including the one who is ill, are dramatic and dangerous. The sick one feels entitled to this attention as compensation for suffering, and is in danger of becoming a tyrant. The primary caregiver(s) feel resentful in spite of their anxiety and concern for the invalid, and the healthy children feel neglected, unloved, and jealous of their sibling. Envying someone who is sick is regarded as sick, so they add guilt to their emotional burden.

It almost seems that change by itself causes loss. Not quite true. The changes instigated by loss cause growth. It doesn't happen without an effort, and there has to be a choice, but there is no growth without change (or pain). The management of change, as I have indicated, is another way of defining the grieving process. Although experts (Toffler, Marris, and any number of pop psychologists) can offer step-by-step directions for the management of change, it's not quite that easy.

For one thing, change keeps changing. *"That was then, this is now"* doesn't quite apply. "That was sometimes, occasionally this is now, but in between I'm not sure," more closely describes the state of inconsistent flux that people experiencing change undergo and must overcome. There are good days and bad days, and there are some days when one would rather not say what kind of day it is.

One woman fought to keep her husband, giving him a long tether through two affairs and one separation only to have him return home and die of cancer. She is a rich woman now because he was still her husband when he died so she got all the insurance money and all the forks. "This is not what I had in mind at all," she says.

Another woman lived through a roller-coaster marriage and six children with a manic-depressive alcoholic who is now making much more money than she is while she scrambles for a living late in life, but she's coping and happier than she's ever been.

Yet another woman was diagnosed with myelogenous leukemia and given six to twelve months to live, who said, "I am not dying of cancer, I am living with it," and who proceeded to travel around the world before she died eight years later.

A man who pays his first wife an enormous amount of alimony left his second wife when she landed an important, time-consuming job, too time-consuming while she settled into it for her to make time for him. He is now living with a devoted young woman but complaining still about how much his first wife is costing him.

Another man has been separated from his wife longer than they have lived together but he still calls on her to accompany him to important public occasions and buys the party booze at Christmas, which he still celebrates with her, living in, but he is free to romp with whomever he likes the rest of the time. As I say, the management of change can lead to growth, but not necessarily.

People make momentous shifts but not the changes they imagine.
—ALICE MUNRO

19. Loss of Friendship

The most fatal disease of friendship is gradual decay, or dislike hourly increased by causes too slender for complaint, and too numerous for removal.
—DR. JOHNSON

"YOU FIND OUT WHO YOUR FRIENDS ARE" — ANOTHER LINE from the Universal Script, oft repeated, by both bereaved and divorced, tells the story of shattered friendships.

People often don't realize that a friendship was fleeting until after a Life Event crumbles it. Couple friends go this route first. Business associates of one's mate, couples one went with to the theater, or bowling, or dancing and drinking (does anyone do that any more?), people who used to invite each other to their Christmas or holiday parties — all these suddenly have short memories when one in their midst becomes single. Divorced men and women usually find out the hard way who got the visiting rights to their friends.

Divorcées and widows may be remembered for coffee or lunch, but their couple friends find them awkward to place at a Noah's Ark dinner table where the place settings come in twos. It has been my observation that most hostesses welcome an extra man at a party, but single men, both divorced and widowed, tell me they have their problems, too. The married men get antsy if a single man talks to their wives too long — the old fox-in-the-chicken-coop syndrome. Singles, male and female, are simply not considered to be part of the fabric of stable society. They have to be paired to be acceptable.

170

Geography makes a big difference in friendship. I have already discussed the mobility of our society and its wide-reaching effects on the nervous system. Friendship is one of its victims, or — perhaps more accurately — neighborliness is. Neighbors often have nothing in common in terms of education, lifestyle, and goals but they give each other mutual cooperation and protection, performing as Block Parents, watching each other's houses, running errands, serving as backup babysitters, sharing work in community plans, uniting in common cause in ratepayers' associations and parents' groups, and providing care in times of personal crisis, that is, telephone watch, food, care and lodging when there is a death in a family, or a new baby, or any major emergency. Unfortunately, this kind of friendship doesn't stretch over the miles and soon dwindles to the Christmas News Bulletin. Even so, one feels the loss.

I used to have a hobby I enjoyed. I used to send people birthday and anniversary cards. I have a poor memory for faces and names but an incredible memory for dates (and good quotations). I used to enjoy selecting and sending cards throughout the year, with notes and jollies (cartoons, mementoes, tea bags, and so on). By the time I stopped to question this hobby, I discovered to my horror that it was costing me more than forty dollars a month. I stopped doing it, not only for financial reasons. I had suffered another kind of loss. I had discovered once again who my friends were.

Slowed for a while by a bad back, I had time to take stock of what I was doing and where I was going again (every loss is accompanied by a gain). That was when I finally faced my painful, irrevocable discovery that I was not number one in anyone's life, that I was alone, I mean *alone*.

The silence of my friends proved it. I discovered that when I sat back (actually, I couldn't sit; I could stand up or lie down). When I did lie down and wait, without reaching out to people, without calling as promised, or suggesting a meeting, or sending a card, very few of them called me. It seemed I had always been the one to make the first move. Why was *I* always the one to call? What would happen if I didn't? I tried it. I stopped calling, I stopped sending cards, and I waited to see what would happen. I found out, once again, who my friends were. I lost a number of "friends." I saved some money and gained some meaningful time. I also discovered more clearly what friendship is all about. Everyone has a different theory.

My theory about friendships is that they last, as a good marriage lasts, when there is a fair trade between the participants.
—JUNE CALLWOOD, *TWELVE WEEKS IN SPRING*

For what is your friend that you should seek him with hours to kill? Seek him always with hours to live. For it is his to fill your need, but not your emptiness.
—KAHLIL GIBRAN, *THE PROPHET*

The moral is not that some friendships die and fade away, it's that some friendships were never true friendships in the first place, and it pays to know the difference. Sometimes it takes the anger of a loss to make this discovery. It's not a pleasant one to make but one conclusion is that real friends must be bound to one's soul with hoops of steel. The other is—it's been said before—that one is one's own best friend.

So far I have been discussing the friends one loses through history and circumstances: distance, death, divorce. Old friends never die, it is said, but they do fade out. One old friend commented to me a long time ago now, "It's easy to make new friends but impossible to make old ones." Time and memory cannot be produced rapidly. The odd thing is that if someone were to meet an old friend as a stranger today, it's unlikely that the two would have much in common. What they do have is a long, intimate knowledge of each other and of each other's families, a very precious continuity. They also have a fierce, protective loyalty. I will never forget the ones who helped me when Bill died, when I had my major surgery, when Matthew had his breakdown, but who also came to my plays and my children's weddings, bought my books, and celebrated my (single) milestones with me. Some friends are more supportive in foul weather than in fair, oddly enough—or is it?

Real friends do not fall by the wayside. If something terrible happens and one of them does, it's like a death. It happened to me recently. I went through the shock, denial, anger, bargaining, and depression, but I have not yet arrived at reconciliation—either with my pain and anger or with my former friend. Even old friendships, though not eroded by time, can be destroyed by betrayal. Once the locks have been changed, the doors stay shut. Beware of bitterness.

The death of a relationship is painful enough and the more ironic because both parties are still alive. That's what happens in separation and divorce: two people are alive on the same planet but dead to each other, yet neither of them will lie down or go away. One hears occasionally of friendships that have surfaced from the wreckage of a marriage. I know of one.

I have not lost a really close friend to physical death — yet — but I have friends who have, and I have some understanding of what that will cost. I hope that I can help when the time comes. One of the most moving accounts of friends supporting a friend in her terminal illness is to be found in June Callwood's book *Twelve Weeks in Spring*, reporting the final days of Margaret Frazer and the care of the people who rallied round and helped her live her dying. At the wake, Callwood said, "We don't have her any more, but we do have our better selves, we have a better sense of the safety of our community. This time the center held." That's important, to hold the center.

Sooner or later, men come between women friends. My father warned me that, when my best friend got married, we would not be as friendly until I got married, too, because marriage made one different. What makes a woman different is not marriage per se but loyalty to her mate. Single women will discuss anything with each other. When only *one* is single, she will continue to confide the problems of her love life to her married friend but the exchange is no longer reciprocal. When one or both are married, a curtain falls between the couple and the world, including the best friend. That constitutes a real loss.

Psychologist Jean Baker Miller thinks it's part of the in-union-there-is-strength, in-division-there-is-power thinking of men regarding women. The policy has certainly kept women from presenting any kind of united front to men for better wages, fairer treatment, equal opportunity. Until only recently it has even kept women silent about their husband's abuse. Loyalty or something keeps their mouths shut. "Many women," comments Miller, "develop a great need to believe they have a strong man to whom they can turn for security and hope in the world." And so they stay silent.

Of course, men will argue that women come between male friends, but usually only when two men want the same woman. Husbands, too, do not discuss their sex life with their male friends. They don't discuss their struggles with the boss at work or their spiritual or financial problems either. That leaves them sports and jokes. Yet all the great friendships in literature have been between men. Why? Because men wrote about them. That, too, will change, and then so, too, will the grieving process for the death of a friend.

Male–female nonsexual friendships have become a phenomenon of these latter decades of the twentieth century, permitted (created?), I think, by the feminist movement, and aided by accessibility. With more and more women working outside the home the chances of their meeting and making friends of the opposite sex increase mightily. These are genuine, heart-warming friendships, and one can be hurt by their loss. Sex, of course, can kill them. I've seen it happen and I've had it happen to me. With any luck, determination, and tact, one can restore some semblance of the past intimacy, but the old carefree trust disappears. No one needs extra sources of pain, and no one learns much from unnecessary grief. I would therefore caution any male or female with a female or male friend, as the case may be, to keep the friendly contact above the waist.

Men need their women friends, more, I would venture to say, than women need their men friends. For most men their closest friend is their wife. That's why they suffer so when she dies. Most men profit by women's friendship and kindness more than they realize.

> Women have served all these centuries as looking-glasses possessing the magic and delicious power of reflecting the figure of man at twice its natural size.
> —VIRGINIA WOOLF, *A ROOM OF ONE'S OWN*

I knew one man well who lost his best friend to cancer. This man does not love women. He's not gay; he enjoys women, but he doesn't love them. His three great loves have been his grandfather, his friend, and his son. When his friend died, I held him and comforted him during one dark night when his soul shuddered at his loss. I was, briefly, his friend.

Men hold women like a scarf across their eyes to protect them from reality (death). As Ernest Becker (*The Denial of Death*) says (one of the few things he says about men or women that I agree with), "Men have to be protected from reality."

This is another aspect of the grieving that is going on in this last decade of the twentieth century. Men and women are grieving the loss of each other — in shock, withdrawal, denial, and anger — and with no acceptance whatever. Grief, remember, is a struggle to recover meaning. If we don't recover meaning, there will be no friendship left between men and women.

VII

DEATH OF POTENTIAL

How do we deal with what might have been? If-only's lead to madness; rue must be worn with a difference; imperfection becomes us all.

20. Dealing With Long-Term Damage

Long ago, when I knew my child was to be permanently retarded, I learned that there are two kinds of sorrow, one which can be assuaged and one which cannot be assuaged.
— PEARL BUCK

SOME GRIEFS DON'T GO AWAY. OF COURSE, NO GRIEF DOES, really. We all know by now that loss is permanent. The lost love object can be internalized, however. Not so with an ongoing grief. It presents a problem that cannot be resolved. We've seen some of that already in the disappearance of a loved one. Now let us consider the damaged one.

I have a damaged child, now an adult. I love him dearly and I will continue to do so all the days of my and his life, but that doesn't mean that I am reconciled to his loss and mine. I just don't dwell on it. That can lead only to madness. I have fought for my son all my life and with a lot of help from others have brought him to a plateau that we can be comfortable with, knowing that there is always the prospect of the next assault. I'm proud of all Matthew has accomplished in spite of his handicap but still constantly fearful for his welfare. I don't often think of what his life and mine would be like if he were normal in the same way that I do not often think of what my life would be like if my husband were still living. Not often, but the thoughts do cross my mind.

I interviewed a woman whose husband had a devastating stroke shortly after they were married and who has cared for him ever since, living in a never-never-land of faithfully married celibacy. I know a man with Alzheimer's disease whose wife is becoming his conscious mind as he loses his. He is losing more memory every day and the loss hurts them both. Her friends offer to "babysit" to give her a break, unconsciously giving her pain with the phrase they use because the man who requires the sitting is no baby. The anguish seems to be never-ending. How does one cope with continuing loss, and with the constant reminders of it? Who cares for the caregivers?

Again, the trick is first to change one's expectations. I learned slowly from Matthew to change my expectations — of all my children. I learned, as many parents I have observed have not, not to demand of any of my children that they be world-beaters. I learned instead to expect them to be the best they could be, doing the best they were capable of, competing with no one. I treasure the essence of the individual. So, too, we must learn to treasure the best in every human being.

The second trick is related to the first, and, that is to treasure the beads, the pearls of solace. My "now" beads, the ones I stored as I gradually became able to bear and then to savor the tolerable moments after my husband's death, are just as important in any long-term threatening/unbearable/untenable situation. Everyone has moments of sheer, irrelevant joy. This capacity for irrelevance is one of the most saving graces human beings possess — another aspect of the riddle. Many of our wryest jokes come out of that irrelevance:

- "I see," said the blind carpenter, as he picked up his hammer and saw.
- "It hurts only when I laugh," says the person with lung cancer.
- "It's a good thing I'm left-handed," says the right-hand amputee.
- "I won't take out any magazine subscriptions," said my father when told he had three months to live.
- "Lady, have you made your donation to the hospital?" I asked myself when I lay alone after surgery with tubes going in and out of every opening in my body. "No," I said to myself, "I give at the orifice." I could have giggled then but it hurt.

Gallows humor. We survive because of it. A friend of mine who had suffered a breakdown and undergone shock treatments, plus endless sessions with a psychiatrist, was back in her swimming group and nervous about somersaulting into the water. "Don't do it," I said, "you've given your head enough trouble already." Everyone else was dismayed at what

I'd said, but my friend laughed. Laughter is a blessing. Perhaps laughter is another name for grace.

Not Grace who? Grace what? Grace under pressure. The *Oxford English Dictionary* defines grace theologically as "the free and unmerited favour of God; the divine influence which operates in men to regenerate and sanctify, and to impart strength to endure trial and resist temptation." I have already mentioned that doctors and other workers in disaster areas have noticed time and again the enormous dignity and courage of victims of incredible calamities. As one doctor put it, "In the midst of all that suffering, I was in the presence of grace." God's love? Also mercy, and pardon. A kind of forgiveness. In the midst of a continuing loss, we must hope for such amazing grace. We can also work at attaining it.

Such thoughts cross the mind of anyone who has to cope with a continuing loss that is still lively and fraught with hazards. A young woman took a deep dive into a shallow pool and didn't come up until someone noticed her lying on the bottom of the pool — paralyzed from the fourth vertebra down — and pulled her out. Her life was changed from that moment but so was her family's, as they not only accommodated to her loss but worked with it. She has recovered more use of her hands than anyone thought possible and has returned to work (teaching) from her electronic wheelchair, living as independently as she can in a special room equipped for her by her parents. Certainly, it crosses people's minds that it would be nice if she had never dived into that pool, but what can they do about it now? Cope.

Cope and count the beads, the blessings. British novelist Paul West and his wife had an enormously damaged child; she was retarded, deaf, autistic, hyperactive, unstable, wearing. In his book about her, West expresses his gratitude to this severely damaged human being, his daughter: "You quicken in us the sense of life and make us grateful for what's usually taken for granted."

One learns to live with damage in oneself in the same way. One of the commonest types for women of late has been mastectomy. Quite apart from the fear of what such surgery implies, a mastectomy is a very personal, continuing loss that threatens one's personhood. "Can a lover bury his face between a lone breast?" asks Sally in British playwright Louise Page's play *Tissue*. That's probably the question that haunts every woman, including Mimi Schwartz , who reports on her mastectomy in the October 1990 edition of *Lear's* magazine. The scar is in her mind, and in her husband's. As Sally says,

> *I will think of this scar, curling across me. Buried in my skin. The vivid crest of the knife gash and the speckling of stitches. When I look in the mirror and think I am looking thinner it will always be right shoulder to the mirror.*
>
> *Then I will turn full frontal and see one breast approaching opulence, I will always notice it curving round me and marking "It was here." I am disgusted. My mark of degradation. It is so humiliating and demanding of attention. I can't think that — if I forget it — the fear will go away.*

Mimi Schwartz describes the slow gavotte of reticence and delicacy she and her husband danced round each other's feelings, she afraid of repeling him, he fearful of hurting her.

> *Last night, I took my gown off in bed, brought his lips to my scar. "My left side needs equal time. It doesn't like being off limits," I announced, as if I were back in the school yard, playing tag. "My pleasure," he said softly, and made me believe that it was.*

I met a woman once who wore glasses with lenses as thick as Coke-bottle bottoms. "But then," she used to say with a shrug, "how much do I want to see?" One of my dearest friends a long time ago was the wife of a minister; she was deaf. She used to turn off her hearing aid before church socials and smile and smile at everyone. How much did she want to hear?

I have a very special friend who is increasingly crippled with multiple sclerosis and who is the sole caregiver for his deaf, Down's syndrome son. Mick has taught Robin considerable mechanical skill, and "the Robin," as he calls him, has become his surrogate muscles. They power each other with love.

I had a friend who walked on the edge of madness most of the time, suffering angry hallucinations and uncharted fear. Her visions were the stuff of poetry. We are all walking wounded.

> Blesser *is a French verb meaning "to wound." In English* bless *means "to confer well-being upon," usually from a divine source (the root of both words means blood). There is a wound in every blessing,*

and it gives pain while it gives grace. That's one of the incredible paradoxes of life.
— THE BOOK OF MATTHEW

Pearl Buck had a retarded child, an unassuagable grief, as she noted. Her husband was mentally incompetent for several years before his death. "For a long time," Buck wrote, "he had not known he was living, and he did not know when he died." When he did die, she had to recall the man he had been before she could begin her grieving.

I have discarded that time of not knowing, When I think of him, I think of him as I knew him, vivid, alive, with infinite variety in thought and word, dominant, invincibly prejudiced in some matters . . . and no intention of changing himself.

Others have told me of this need to go back in time, to remember the whole person who disappeared some months or years before rather than think about the weak, sick, wizened, cruelly crippled person who finally dies. In fact, sometimes it takes a conscious effort of will to forget the last impressions and that death mask and to revive memory's picture of the loved one in health and wholeness. This is the kind of envisioning my grandfather did when he looked at my tiny, pale grandmother in her coffin. I have had women tell me how hard it was to mourn the last body and face they remember, that they have to cast that image from their minds and conjure up the other one, the one they fell in love with.

"They say the owl was a baker's daughter. Lord, we know what we are, but know not what we may be," said poor, mad Ophelia. We keep working at it, though, keep finding out what we may be, through loss and damage and pain. We keep working at it, at others, most of all at ourselves. Every loss is accompanied by a gain. We just have to keep looking for it.

182

21. Chosen Losses

Alternatives, and particularly desirable alternatives,
grow only on imaginary trees.
— SAUL BELLOW

A STORY BY JACK FINNEY POSTULATES A SECOND WORLD that exists beside the one we live in, the world of the Other Choice. If one had taken the other job, married the other person, moved to the other house, what would life today be like? The Other Choice could be lived easily enough because it almost was, it might have been, it was that close but for the toss of a coin or whatever means was used to make the decision.

There are entry points to this other world, the hero of Finney's novel discovers, and his is a corner newsstand where, once he has collected enough coins with the faces of *other* presidents on them — a Dewey quarter, a Wilkie dime, a Stevenson nickel, whatever — he can buy a paper and go up the street to his alternate life.

I've often thought of that image and wondered about those other choices, whether, in fact, they still exist somewhere, as Finney suggests. Though our lives have been affected mightily by the turnings we did make and the roads we did travel, still we carry our knowledge and memory of the ways not taken, and our reasons for not taking them. In a way, we have incorporated some of the other choices within our present psyches. If death did not result (this is all highly hypothetical), if the other choice would not have meant death, then its effect has remained partly within us. It's like an alternate world.

What if death did result? There is no bargaining with a choice once made. Several people have written about their choice to help a loved one die. This, surely, is a heavy choice that hangs like a millstone around one's neck, ready to sink one with the weight of it. All the rationalization and self-justification in the world and "all the perfumes of Arabia will not sweeten this . . . hand." Once we have accepted the freedom — no, the necessity — of choice, then we must accept the responsibility as well. This is the hard edge of acceptance, nothing soft or passive about it. We make our choices, then we live with them.

Often we are stampeded into a bad choice. It would be wise to remember Toffler's advice for managing change and not allow ourselves to be rushed. Widows, for example, shouldn't consider moving for at least a year following their bereavement, if they can possibly help it. They don't know who they are yet. Widowers would do well to remain unmarried for at least a year, for the same reason. Divorce settlements are often hastily and unfairly cobbled by undue pressures. It doesn't make sense to make a binding, unilateral decision about one's life and the lives of one's children at a time of great stress such as the upheaval that marks a divorce. The best settlement I ever heard of was that of American writer Mary Kay Blakely who made a divorce agreement designed to expire at regular intervals so that the situation could be reassessed and renegotiated.

Most of us live with a subconscious awareness of our alternatives and a speculative curiosity about our lives: if we had made the other choice, married the other person, had the baby, moved away, asked for a divorce, accepted the job offer, what would have happened? Obviously, not all the choices we actually made were the best ones. We have all made mistakes. If we had known then what we know now, would we have made the same choices? Who knows? Such conjecture doesn't do any one any good. Whether or not they were mistakes, we have to live with our decisions and learn from them, take it from there.

One of the choices women have been making in the last decade or so is beginning to bother some of them. Whoever coined the phrase "biological clock" must have been aware of its ominous ticking, counting off the time during which a woman's body can safely bear a healthy baby. A significant number of women have left it too late, or almost.

Having chosen career over marriage, or, if married, career over motherhood, women in their mid- and late thirties, early forties, now find themselves ticking past maternity as they realize belatedly that they'd really like to have a baby.

I have already mentioned the trauma of abortion. What of the decision itself, the choice, whether by omission or commission, not to have a baby? Obviously, it's one of the most disturbing choices a woman can make (or be forced to make), and one that lives on as an if-only in her life.

Funny: as we go down the if-only road of thinking we tend to think that the other path would have been the better one. If only we had done this, then life would have been better. If-only's are like the fish that got away: the farther they recede into our memory, the bigger and better they get. We wipe away the guns and knives and barriers that seemed to us at the time to make the choice clear, or impossible, as the case might have been. We often forget that when faced with a choice between two evils we simply chose the lesser evil at the time. Margaret Mead once commented that abortion was the lesser of two evils; that, when we finally get smart enough, it will become a choice that will never have to be made, because there will never be conceived an unwanted child. We're nowhere near that smart yet.

Later, looking back, when time and circumstances have erased or softened the edges of the choice we made, we look at the other one, the path not chosen, strewn now, we think, with primroses, and we sometimes regret the decision. We have to remember the sequence of events that led us to it and the essential difference between self-sacrifice and self-preservation. I teeter on the brink of a huge moral discussion, so I will withdraw before I lose my balance.

Choice is a relatively new experience for women, historically speaking, and one that is not being granted without a fight. The female's right to her own body is still being fought in the courts and the Old Boys' Clubs, and it's still not guaranteed. Women's bodies are still in danger of being nationalized, like parks. Small wonder that doubt and regret have played such a large part in women's choices; they haven't been getting much support.

Psychologist Carol Gilligan, in her landmark book *In a Different Voice*, reports on an abortion study she made to analyze and assess women's choices and their reactions to them. Gilligan pointed out the need and the aptness of her study: "The availability of choice, and with it the onus of responsibility, has now invaded the most private sector of the woman's domain." Birth control and abortion have given women the means of effecting their choice; they do not, however, control their reactions. Women know that what they do affects not only their own lives but those of others around them. It's hard enough to accept responsibility for one's own choices, even harder to accept awareness of what those choices do to other people. Abortion forces this responsibility and awareness.

In any case, we now see women who are grieving for their babies that never were nor ever will be. Isn't that a strange kind of grief — for something that never happened? Perhaps not so strange. Psychologist Robert Ornstein says that "the non-occurrence of a desired event may be stressful." In fact, it may have a profound effect on a life — or two lives.

At whatever age one decides that one has made a foolish choice, most of the time it's not too late to try again, to withdraw the self and rediscover other aspects of it. Even if it's too late to have a child of one's own flesh and blood, it is still possible to adopt one. With a heart that's big enough, one can reach out to a lot of children through various kinds of volunteer or paid work with children. I have seen several women who took early retirement to throw themselves into community work, helping out at women's hostels or teaching young unwed teenaged mothers.

There is more danger of despair than of anger in some of the choices people make. Self again (always) is involved. The loss of control over one's life causes an overwhelming feeling of helplessness. Men, particularly, who have been accustomed to (think they have) more control over their lives, feel devastated by the discovery of their own powerlessness; women tend to give in more gracefully (or is it merely resignation?), but they, too, will feel despair. I remember writing in my diary at a crucial moment of my life: "I don't conduct my life; it drags me along behind it."

Being helpless and out of control means we have lost any ability to predict what will happen next. If we could, we would be able to manipulate events to our own liking. When events are unpredictable because beyond our control, then life itself becomes meaningless. The loss of meaning is a terrible source of grief. That way lies terror. Without control there is no predictability, without predictability no meaning, without meaning no survival. This is more change, more loss than one's psyche can survive. If life is to continue, meaning must be established, the thread of continuity must be picked up again to guide us out of the Minotaur's maze. "Have a reason to get out of bed in the morning," is advice I have been giving myself for years — and anyone else who will listen.

The reason changes; the conscious choice does not. People often find their life work through the Life Event that left them staggering in their tracks, and the first thing they discover is that they weren't on track at all, they were in a rut. We have to remember that choice is not not always getting what we chose but choosing what we get.

I have heard and read countless stories of people who found their life's work and meaning in their life's most devastating blow. There's a widower who began self-help groups for other widowers but, since he realized men hate to attend such sob-sessions, he presented them in the form of poker games. There's that man who helped his wife die at her request who has since started a world-wide organization plugging euthanasia. There is the father of a quadraplegic who designed a van for his daughter to be able to transport her comfortably and who is now in business selling models of it to others similarly afflicted. There are all those parents of the learning disabled and mentally handicapped, so many of whom I have met in the course of my son Matthew's life, who give their services and support to the volunteer groups that make their kids' lives so much richer. And there's me, trying to comfort others with the slivers of wisdom I have scratched from my own soap-opera life. As my husband used to say, if you get a lemon, make lemonade.

22. Imperfection and Mortality

And so they lived happily ever after . . .
— GRIMM'S FAIRY TALES

WHAT WENT WRONG? WHAT HAPPENED TO THE BRAVE NEW world, the American Dream, the Canadian Sunset? Why didn't God/ Mother/Father/Madison Avenue keep those promises? If we went to church regularly and loved our neighbors, ate our greens and helped with the dishes, toed the line and did the right thing, used a deodorant daily and drank the Classic cola, we were supposed to be safe, loved, popular, protected, healthy, and maybe even immortal. But it hasn't been like that at all. What went wrong?

Part of the problem has to do with our expectations. We are addicted to perfection, as Marion Woodman illustrates in her wonderful book so titled (*Addiction to Perfection*). We seem to have learned from somewhere, been told by someone, that if we try hard enough we will be perfect. We have to try because no one will love us if we aren't perfect. Be polite, don't sulk, be punctual, don't fart, use the right fork, smile, wear the right clothes, stay skinny, stay young, be multi-orgasmic, be one of the beautiful people. "You can never be too rich or too thin," as the Duchess of Windsor used to say. No one will love you if you're fat, poor, old, ugly, or gray. No one would love you at all if they knew what you're really like, so don't tell. Keep it secret.

The fault is not in our stars and certainly not with our mothers and fathers, for they had their own problems. The deficiency is within ourselves: we allow others to take away our sense of self. We've created a set of golden idols and ignored the internal commandments. As for all those golden idols — money, marriage, children, money, job, house, car, travel, money, food/wine/entertainment, love, money, and perfection — since when isn't too much enough? Since never. Even if we had it all, it never lasts. In the wink of an eye it's gone. Death spoils it all.

Even before the grief comes, the rage is there. All grief does is rip away the veil that shielded us from reality. Some shield. Don't do me any more favors.

Am I advising anyone to be grateful for grief? Perhaps I am, if that's the only road to reality. Once the veil is lifted, we are free not to be perfect, but to be wounded. We can permit pain and allow for imperfection (and creation). Lewis Thomas, that sensitive scientist who became a Pulitzer prize–winning man of letters, has commented that, without error, there would be no progress. He points out that discoveries happen by accident and he gives illustrations from the world of science. So with creativity. Creation is an accident; it is the pearl in the oyster, produced by an initial irritation, a *flaw*. Without imperfection there would be no creation. The pearl is "of great price" as the line goes. So is creation — of great price. It costs. Unless we're forced, we seem absolutely unable or unwilling to pay the price. It was so much easier to be unconscious.

Rich, thin, strong, beautiful, fat, we tumble toward eternity and try to ignore fading beauty and the smile-sliding wrinkles of age. Death comes inexorably along, sooner or later, not ours but that of someone we love more dearly than life itself, as they say, or think we do, and here we are again, out in the cold and dark, alone, unloved, and not one bit attractive. What do we do now?

Look in the mirror.

Grief is a two-way mirror, like the abyss Nietzsche described: "When you look into the abyss the abyss looks into you." Suddenly, irrevocably, face to face with ourselves, we look and see reality, no tidy superficial perfection but reality with all its unsightly knobs and cutting edges. It hurts — a lot. Perfection was never like this. Funny thing is, fewer people survive perfection than survive reality.

Sooner or later the mirror of perfection shatters and powders into glass and, when we swallow it (the myth), the gleaming lethal shards slice our insides to red ribbons of uncertainty. However, the two-way mirror of grief enables us, if we can stand it and look at it long enough, to step through it. We come out on the other side of that looking glass into the world of nothing. I am reminded of Martin Gardner's comments (in *The Annotated Alice*) on the world of anti-matter on the other side of the mirror. Alice, it may be remembered, held her cat, Dinah, up to the mirror and wondered if the milk on the other side of the mirror would be good to drink. Gardner says that it would make her explode. Mirrors are not to be fooled with. As I say, on the other side of the mirror of grief is no-thing.

Through no-thing it is possible to achieve at-one-ment. *Atonement*. According to the *Oxford English Dictionary*, atonement means "the condition of being *at one* with others; concord; agreement." On a theological level it is "reconciliation or restoration of friendly relations between God and sinners . . . variously used by theologians in the sense of *reconciliation, propitiation, expiation*." We have to remember that there's no making up for something if there's no something to be made up for. There has to be a loss, someone's loss. Then all it costs is grief and all it wins is self. Hard-won!

It shall little profit a person to gain the world and lose one's soul. We've heard that line before, or something like it. Eye of the needle and all that. The other prophets send a similar message. Worldly goods are just not worth all that trouble. Why doesn't anyone seem to believe it, or take it to heart? Almost everyone we know is running around trying to gain the world, or a corner of it. Not all of us fool around with power politics, or oil or nerve chemicals or the Bomb. On a smaller scale, though, we hammer nails into earth's coffin pursuing our own expensive version of perfection: the perfect house beautiful, the priceless perfect private collection of something or other, the perfect pasta, the unassuming perfect wine, the perfect trip with its perfect mountain and perfect sunset. Our search for amusing trivia is relentless and becomes almost an end in itself. The end is perfection, unattainable perfection, which doesn't mean we don't try to attain it. "Addiction to perfection," says Marion Woodman, "is an end in itself." It is not, I hope, a suicidal addiction.

> *Mirror, mirror, on the wall,*
> *Who's the sexiest of them all?*

Sex is one of the panaceas a lot of people seek comfort from in time of loss, some reassurance that they are still alive, still desirable, not alone. When the suddenly single "go foolish," sex becomes another addiction. One searches for self in the one-way mirror of a lover's eyes, giving up one's body to a demon lover in the attempt to find (or avoid) self. It's one of the manifestations of grief, part of the searching pattern. It can take quite a beguiling time to get over. For a while, quite a while, a lover can be as electric as a blanket. The problem is, the controls are on the other side. For a while, it's another way to avoid reality.

What about that reason to get out of bed every morning? What about the future and all the plans we made? The catch is that the future won't hold still for planning. "Life," as many people have said, "is what happens when we were planning other things." So is death. One cannot put death on hold, cannot file it tidily away in a drawer or in a notebook, to be pulled out at maturity (age-ninety-six/jealous-husband time) and cashed in. Death is what happens to all our plans for perfection, and it's a good thing, for without it we'd all be Struldbrugs, and a farther cry from perfection one could not be as horrified to see. Struldbrugs, remember, were the immortals in Jonathan Swift's third book in *Gulliver's Travels*.

Gulliver was excited at the thought of meeting immortals. He thought they must be "happiest beyond all comparison . . . being born exempt from that universal calamity of human nature, have their minds free and disengaged, without the weight and depression of spirits caused by the continual apprehension of death." He saw Struldbrugs as the source of "wise counselling and instruction in the wisdom of former ages." Who would not want to live forever? He discovered, however, that in Luggnagg the appetite for living forever was not so keen, with the awful example of the Struldbrugs constantly before them.

Gulliver mistakenly supposed an immortality based on eternal youth and vigor. (All of us, according to another survey, lock in at a certain age that we see ourselves as, no matter how chronologically old we grow. Most of us are about thirty-five. A corollary to this is the observation by the Countess Metternich, that "old age is 15 years older than I am.") Struldbrugs, Gulliver found, don't die, but they don't stay young either. They acquire all the irritable qualities and infirmities of the old and direct their envy at the vices of the young, which they can no longer indulge in, and the deaths of the old, which they have been denied. They forget wisdom and experience. The happiest among them seem to be those who lose their memories and who slip into helpless dotage; however, without memory they cannot read or talk or entertain themselves. After he had seen them, Gulliver wished he could send a couple of Struldbrugs to his own country, "to arm our people against the fear of death."

Immortality is not really anyone's lifestyle. Nor is perfection, no matter how hard we aspire to it. I remember that joke, "Death is nature's way of telling us to slow down." Perhaps grief is death's way of telling us we aren't perfect. Our wounds mar us, our scars destroy our perfect symmetry.

Let us give thanks.

VIII

RENEGOTIATION

No bargains. No deals. But a reconciliation, nonetheless.
Coming to terms with the harsher clauses of life's contract.
It's tough and it takes thought, time after time.

23. Coming to Terms

So farewell hope, and with hope,
Farewell fear.
— JOHN MILTON

"WHAT'S THE WORST THAT CAN HAPPEN?" PEOPLE WILL ASK, trying to help friends walk through a potentially bad scenario. The question is supposed to make one realize that most worries are really quite trivial; the worst *doesn't* happen, most of the time. When the worst *does* happen, that's when to start worrying. By then, it's too late anyway. Once death has happened, for example, one can dare anything.

I compared the loss of my husband to a hostage system gone awry. Bill was my biggest hostage to Fate, the love that made me most vulnerable to loss. Once death took him, I was no longer as vulnerable to external circumstances. Granted, there are other hostages, other people dear to my heart whose deaths would sadden me. But now that the worst has happened, Fate does not have me by the throat, nor ever will again. No fear — a lot less, anyway.

Grief does that. Life here on the other side of the mirror isn't as introspective or frightening as it was back when there was everything to lose. Looking back through the mirror from this side is even, at times, exhilarating. I can see others more clearly now that I don't have to watch myself all the time. I know where I am now — most of the time. I'm right here, inside me, where I belong.

And yet I am forever off balance. "The wounded healer" is a common title given now to workers in palliative-care units, in bereaved family groups, in widows' and widowers' networks, and in all the support systems predicated on loss and devoted to recovery. The idea is that the healer has to have experienced the wound first-hand in order to understand and to help others. It takes one to know one. You have to have been there. And the halt shall lead the blind. I carry my healed wound as a constant blessing.

Like Jacob, all of us have wrestled with the angel of death and been wounded. If we were smart or lucky, we asked for and received the angel's blessing, as Jacob did. Thus wounded and thus blessed, we walk, perhaps with a limp, but erect and proud, identifying ourselves by the wry grin we wear like a badge; we're survivors. We have, in short, come to terms with our loss.

Grief experts — psychologists, psychiatrists, social workers — speak of "renegotiating" the loss. Further, they point out the necessity for the young to go through the renegotiating process several times as they get older and as their perspective changes. The loss of a parent keeps changing in significance and dimension as a child gathers experience and new insights. One day a good nine years after my husband's death, I walked by my son Matt's bedroom while he was playing tapes. George Harrison's "My Sweet Lord" drifted through the door and I heard Matt say, "My sweet Lord, why did you have to take my dad?" I knocked at the door and asked my son if he'd like to talk about it. We have to do that, keep talking about it, because it — it being our relationship to the loss and to the lost one — keeps changing, even as we change.

I read somewhere when I was first widowed that I had to develop a new relationship with my husband, that it would keep changing. I tried to accept the idea but I didn't understand it. It had no validity for me. He was gone and I missed him terribly, that was all I knew. Little by little, though, he crept inside me ("no bigger than a moth") and nestled there. The only time I actually talk out loud to him is when I get lost, which I do frequently. I know other widows who shout at their husbands when things break and their Mr. Fixit has left them to cope with the repairs. I also know widows — and widowers — whose late spouse comes to bed with their new lover/mate, and sometimes (they've told me) they can't reach a climax because of it.

Quite eerie, that. It happened to me once, and my absence was noted. "Hey, where did you go?" my significant friend asked. Out. I thought of Scarlett O'Hara dreaming of Ashley Wilkes while in Rhett Butler's arms and his cursing her "cheating little soul." I guess I don't blame him. It would be wise, I think, for the bereaved or the divorced to be very clear in their minds about whom they are sleeping with, but I do admit that sometimes it's not that easy to tell. We are such victims of hit-and-run memories.

Fortunately, new memories intervene, new memories of the old love. I live now in a cottage by a lake, very much alone, with only nine other occupied households on the shore in the winter, and a wonderful view of trees and water from my studio windows. Obviously, my husband never saw this place; I moved in fourteen years after his death. But, late one winter day, I drove home from Toronto before the sun was gone and rushed into the house and straight through to the deck to put out fresh sunflower seeds for my birds because I'd been gone for three days and I knew they'd been asking for me and, as I stood there gazing out at them from the deck door, I felt Bill's presence, clearly, behind me. I felt it so strongly that I turned and looked down the hall to the back door with the late-afternoon sun slanting in through its window, with only motes dancing in the sunlight. No Wylie wraith. He was there, all the same, and I knew it, and I felt — how can I put it? — so grateful and so loved, still. As I say, we renegotiate our relationship with the dead. If we're lucky, the relationship continues to be a comfort.

"If you don't give your first wife a place in your life, she may creep up from time to time and want to know where she belongs, like a ghost that wants to be remembered." One would have to know that's a widower speaking, because he has remarried. Even so, the first wife retains a significant place in his life. A conversation with any widow or widower will produce a similar comment.

Keith Johnstone is a drama teacher at the University of Calgary who has written a book for actors that I refer to every time I go to write a new play. In *Impro* (short for "improvisation") Johnstone offers a fine piece of advice for actors who play Theatresports (Johnstone's invention, kind of Second City–type improvs) when they're too far into a story or a line of thought and don't know how to continue. "When in doubt," he says, "look back, and reconnect."

It should be evident how useful the advice is to a playwright but it's also remarkably valuable to anyone who has suffered a loss. As one progresses farther and farther into the grieving process and is, in fact, did one but know it, not far from acquiescence (the other side of the looking glass), one hits panic. This is the full, staggering knowledge (it takes a while) that *life will never be the same again*. Actually, one passes this signpost several times but the distance information is different each time:

"POINT OF NO RETURN"

or maybe:

8 km or 3 months,

whichever comes first.

So here we are again, at that crucial, recurring point. Others have recognized it too. This, from a widow I interviewed:

"It is impossible to be as we were before."

And this, from a bereaved parent who wrote me:

"I now realize one never does get back to normal, but that we are changed forever by our loss."

Of course, one will never be the same again; of course, one cannot turn back time, or go back. I should have realized that. Why don't I ever learn? (It's not that I don't; it's that I have to keep on learning the same thing over and over again.) But one can look back. *Look back, and reconnect* — in other words, renegotiate the loss. We have to return to the point of wounding, and connect again. Each time we go, we take someone new with us, the new (changing) self we have become. Each time we go, we understand more clearly.

"We really begin to understand something," says psychologist Jean Baker Miller, "only *after* we have already begun to change it — a symptom, a character trait, a way of living."

Grief is a symptom, not a cause (change or loss is the cause); the character trait is authenticity; the way of living is life after death — all very different! In reconnecting with the point of pain and renegotiating the relationship with the person lost, we possess the past, and acknowledge *now*.

That was then, this is now. Now is all any of us has. Right now is okay.

24. Coping and Problem Solving

I've developed a new philosophy. . . . I only dread one day at a time.
— CHARLIE BROWN

SIX YEARS AGO I WAS ANGRY. I HAD BEEN RUNNING VERY hard for a dozen years since my husband's death and I felt broke and tired and betrayed and lonely and angry, for all I looked successful and my married friends said they envied me. I decided to seek sanctuary, a quiet place to work and finally heal.

To do so I had to sell my urban residence since I couldn't afford to own two establishments. The place I finally found was very small. I had to get rid of more of my possessions in order to squeeze into my rural retreat, though I had lightened my load considerably when I moved from the family home of my Other Life to the apartment in Toronto. By this time my children were old enough to receive things for their own homes. What they didn't want I managed to unload, mainly on charity bazaars and flea markets as I didn't have a garage to have a garage sale in. It takes an adult lifetime to amass such a load of stuff; it took time and organization to get rid of everything: public auctions and carloads and moving vans and private sales through newspaper ads.

From the time my big place sold until I found and moved to the cottage, I lived for a year and a half in a rented two-room apartment in a high-rise while I dispersed the accumulation of a lifetime, systematically stripping myself of possessions (except my books). The night my bedroom furniture left the big apartment, I sat on the empty bedroom floor and went through all the mementoes of my life: scrapbooks and boxes full of theater programs, souvenirs, letters, cards, menus, on and on — even a ration book from the Second World War. I drank wine and got totally maudlin, reliving my life and tossing out most of it. It took me several nights. Each morning I dragged great green garbage bags stuffed with memories down the hall to the garbage room. It was a traumatic time.

From the moment the big apartment was sold, I started to develop a pain in my lower back and right hip and down my leg. It got worse, to the point that I couldn't sit. I lay down or I stood up. What writing I could do I did standing up at a table with a couple of phone books raising my paper to writing level. I sought relief from my doctor who prescribed a brief course of muscle relaxants, an orthopedic surgeon (nothing showed on X-rays), a strange nerve-lady, an acupuncturist, a very bad chiropractor who made it worse, and a miracle man (another chiropractor) who worked hard to get me straightened out, and succeeded.

By that time I had figured out what I had done, and I worked hard to cooperate. I am convinced we play massive puns on our bodies (while still agreeing with Susan Sontag that illness is not a metaphor). What I was doing was *dragging my foot, keeping one leg/foot in the other room of my life* as I prepared to take this giant step of change into a wholly different lifestyle. No wonder my hip and leg hurt!

When I realized what it/I was all about, I canceled all engagements and locked myself into my tiny high-rise space for an entire weekend to work through it. I more or less fasted, drinking herbal teas and juices. I did some intensive journalling, writing, almost stream-of-consciousness stuff, to get at what was bothering me, and I did a lot of body-work: free-form dancing (with that stiff, sore leg) to such music as Pachelbel's "Canon" and Handel's "Sheep May Safely Graze." After that weekend I told my chiropractor to do his best because I *was* going to get better. And I did. That's coping. That's also a good chiropractor.

When one is locked into stiff, tight, painful, intensive grief, body-work helps a lot. Just to move and begin to bend out all that resistance is an effective beginning. Women are uptight and self-conscious enough about this sort of activity at the best of times, and men will absolutely rebel at the thought (all right, then, play squash!), but both should try to keep an open mind about it. A massage would be effective for both genders.

Good nutrition is vitally important for both genders, too, in fact, all-round good health habits are essential. When first on their own, women tend to eat tea and toast, easy, no-fuss-why-bother-when-it's-only-me cooking for one. Men alone tend to eat out, taking their big meal at noon on business, and if they stay in for the evening, they settle, as did one divorced man I know, for a bowl of cereal heavy on the cream and sugar. No one can be blamed for reverting to comfort foods in times of stress but it's not wise to overdo them. Comfort food tends to be loaded with the carbs and sugar — or salt, depending on the comfortee's taste buds. I don't know many people who turn to a crunchy, crisp, fresh salad as a comfort food. It's too noisy. Most people like something soft and creamy and bland and nonthreatening. Another phrase for comfort food is nursery food; people revert to their childhood foods: nice, soft, unchallenging pap. Well and good, up to a point. When there is a knot in the stomach and a lump in the throat, I'll go along with any food that will slide down without a protest and nourish the body a bit. I remember about a week after Bill died, a friend sent over some freshly grilled chicken and I actually ate a drumstick, the first food I'd eaten in a week. Later, another friend sent over a custard and I liked that. As I say — comfort food.

Soon, however, attention has to be paid to nutrition habits and other health needs. When one is so vulnerable emotionally and so tired, resistance runs low and one is susceptible to illness. Sleeping patterns, as already noted, are impossible; lack of sleep contributes to the risk of getting seriously run down. I don't approve of sleeping pills. They're a crutch, as are tranquilizers. If tranquilizers are to be used, then they should be taken in conjunction with therapy or counseling, not by themselves. Warm milk at bedtime calms the nerves and induces sleep. Camomile tea always knocks me out. Regular exercise each day and/or a walk before or after dinner will also aid sleep. If the body is relaxed and tired enough, perhaps it can pull the mind in after it. I write in my journal at night (and in the morning too) and plan the next day, but some people find such planning makes them tense and they prefer something more remote from their own lives. Some people read something before they sleep, usually a few pages of a novel. A few pages of the Bible or a brief browse through something tender or reflective can help. About six months into my bereavement I found a book of spiritual meditations that helped me a lot, and I read and reread it, starting again at the beginning the minute I finished it. It led me into meditation and all sorts of useful mental and emotional control. For those so inclined, I do recommend meditation.

Perhaps solitary meditation and a retreat into self are coping methods that are too far down the line for most people still struggling through the daily logistics of grief. Many turn to support groups to reassure themselves, first, that they are *not* alone in their woes, and second, that they are *not* going insane. The widow-to-widow program first developed at Harvard University by Dr. Phyllis Silverman is based on the idea that no one can help as can someone who has already experienced a similar loss. There are two parts to this program: one is a volunteer, one-on-one, buddy system, the kind of talk and companionship that families and friends used to provide before we all left home and lost our maps and our way. The other part is a group program, scheduled meetings at which widows can share with each other not only their anger and fear but also common-sense tips and financial advice.

Widowers' programs set up on the same format initially were not as successful because men traditionally don't want to talk about their feelings; they'd rather *do* something. New kinds of groups — not different groups — but a different structure and format for men have proved more successful.

Dr. Herbert Gerjoy is credited as the person who saw "situational grouping" as a way of recognizing and organizing people going through changes. By being grouped according to the life circumstance they are going through, people caught in a maelstrom of change can be supported by people in a similar situation. There are now more than half a million support groups in North America attended by more than fifteen million people — at least once a month, if not more frequently, up to a couple of times a week. (Alcoholics Anonymous still recommends attendance at ninety meetings in the first three months.) Support is offered to anyone who is undergoing "transitional difficulties" — people who share a common pain, from death of one's spouse, being battered and battering, Alzheimer's, schizophrenia in a close relative, mastectomies, murder of one's child, incest, PLWAs (Persons Living with AIDS), alcoholism, rape, on and on and on. Based on the idea "you had to be there," support groups offer the hands-on experience of others working through the same problems.

Support groups are the ultimate in self-help, with all the concomitant dangers. The chief danger is of bad advice. I am told that specific instructions are not encouraged. As in dream groups, which I have been in, one develops an instinct as to the value of what someone is saying. I mean, people can usually tell if it's nonsense.

Ideally, a support group should self-destruct, or at least have a very high turnover in its membership. If not, it's in danger of becoming an introspective, self-imposed ghetto. The goal of a support group, after all, is the mental health and recovery of its members. If the self-help therapy is successful, the person no longer needs the support of the group. *Self*-support is the goal and the achievement.

We're on our own again.

Conclusion

Learn to lose in order to recover, and remember that nothing stays the same for long, not even pain, psychic pain. Sit it out. Let it all pass. Let it go.

— MAY SARTON

IN THIS BOOK I HAVE BEEN DISCUSSING THE EFFECTS OF LOSS and the management of the changes it causes without ever touching on how to change change; to do that seems impossible. The phrase "circumstances beyond our control" says it all. It presents us with unyielding results, and we simply have to cope as best we can. Even coping doesn't come easily.

We have to respond to life's events by being responsible, not by hiding. We know that; we learned that in Grade Six. We have to be *honest* and confront the loss without trying to find an immediate substitute. We understand that it's unhealthy to repress our grief or pretend we weren't *that* hurt. We are aware that we must try to *withdraw our emotional investment* and recover our self from the lost object so that we can be not quite whole again, but healed.

In other words, *we* have to change. So how can we manipulate Life Events when we are the ones who have been forced by them to change?

I watched one woman do this. Married, with three young children, she lost her way of life and all her comfortable assumptions when her husband, a successful professional, was killed in a car accident (there was some suggestion that if the emergency ward had acted more quickly with blood transfusions he might have lived — always the waste, always the if-only). She staggered at first (we all do). She moved with her children away from her home town (never easy), gave herself a course in grief psychology, started to write, and is now conducting support seminars for the newly bereaved. She changed her own life; now she's changing others'.

Another woman whose murdered adult daughter died in her arms is now trying to ease the pain for other bereaved parents, working through Bereaved Families of Ontario (BFO, an active support organization with fifteen affiliates in Ontario). All the bereaved parents involved in BFO, in fact, are incredibly dedicated to sharing their pain and lightening the load for others.

Once a person has gathered strength within and no longer feels fearful or unable to cope, the effects of Life Events are more easily dealt with. The power to control a situation lies not only in our perception of what has happened but also in our perception of ourselves. Some things, like death, of course, cannot be changed, but we can transform our attitude to it.

Here are some things people who have confronted loss and who are coming or have come through it have to say:

- "It is strange how we, or some of us, can eventually walk away alone quite contented, from a person who was once so very dear in our lives."
- "Wisdom was easier before the fact, of course. There remains the living to do afterwards."
- "The trick to survival is how we choose to face the future. We can either wallow in our grief or we can get on with life. But one thing we can be sure of, and that is that we will never be the same again."
- "I didn't like seeing my son's tools or using them. Initially I would carefully clean them and return them to exactly the same spots in the toolbox drawers, as if I were borrowing them. In time I forced myself to call them mine and arrange them my way."
- "My advantage is being diabetic. Diabetics must eat, properly, and on time, thereby avoiding a common aspect of bereavement: lack of nourishment."
- "Three years ago I joined a Parents' (really Mothers') Support Group, and we have become very very fast friends."
- "We came here to the lake and when my husband played golf every

day I would grieve for maybe two or three hours — 'keening' — all alone so no one knew, although my husband did."

- "It's not time that heals you but what you do with that time."

Others before me have commented on the paradox life hands us: that we must lose a life to find ourselves, that we must let go in order to possess anything. It seems that paradox is another survival tool. Viktor Frankl reports that he can ease people's insomnia by paradoxical intention. When someone comes to him complaining of sleeplessness, Frankl challenges the person. He instructs his patient to stay awake and keep track of the hours he is wakeful. Usually his patient, consciously fighting sleep in order to track his wakeful moments, falls asleep.

A mother uses the same technique with an irritable child. "Don't laugh," she says. "Whatever you do, don't laugh. Your socks are dirty, you're tired and hungry, you certainly don't feel like laughing because your eyes are wonky and your stomach is rumbling. Growl, growl — don't laugh!" By this time the child is off into paroxysms of giggles.

We can use paradoxical intention on ourselves. By giving ourselves not just the freedom but an order to panic, to go ahead and have an anxiety attack, to rant and howl and cry and get hysterical, we actually manage to calm down. Once I took a poet to a retreat where I used to write, a friend's farm deep in the country. My writer friend had been recently released from a psychiatric hospital after an acute anxiety attack and she was very hyper, restless, pacing, and angry at me and the world. I took her out on the deck of the farmhouse and invited her to howl with me, to screech her rage at the crows. Two wild shrieks and we were both giggling and feeling much better. We went for a quiet walk. Not that a couple of paradoxical screams cured my poor friend, but she did feel better for a time, and so did I. These are short-term treatments, however. A major shift is required to deal with the change that smashed a hole in life as we knew it.

When something terrible has happened and we face the prospect of long-term suffering, we have to deal directly with what the event has done and is doing to us. It requires our full consciousness and no evasion. Greater minds than mine have struggled with the problem of pain.

Walter M. Miller's haunting classic novel *A Canticle for Leibowitz* was first published in 1959; the 1988 Bantam edition I bought to reread had already gone through fifteen printings. The theology is probably a bit biased but it's not why I remembered this book for so long. What stuck was its attempt to deal with the problem of pain and its statement of the meaning of suffering.

At the end of the story, which takes place several centuries from now, the worst holocaust of them all is finally going to destroy the planet. Across the road from a monastery that has been the focus of the book, the army has set up an emergency euthanasia station for lethally affected radiation victims. The current abbot condemns the program to the doctor in charge of the unit, calling it "state-sponsored suicide." The doctor argues that it's better than letting people "die horribly by degrees." Better? the abbot challenges the doctor. Less public spectacle? Less horror?

More merciful, the doctor means. "If you think you have a soul that God would send to Hell if you chose to die painlessly instead of horribly, then go ahead and think so," he says.

The abbot explains. "You don't *have* a soul, Doctor. You *are* a soul. You *have* a body temporarily." That's the crux of the argument.

Later the abbot argues specifically with a woman and her little girl who have been given their tags entitling them to die. He tells them that their pain should be offered to God. The mother is appalled at the thought that God would be pleased at her baby's pain.

Not the pain, the priest explains, but the endurance. "In spite of bodily afflictions . . . pain . . . is often a temptation to despair, anger, loss of faith." Even the ancients, the abbot points out, knew that one could bear anything nature dishes out. An aside: This is true. We only have to recall Paul's letter to the Corinthians:

> For God will not try you beyond what you are able but together with the trial will give you the strength to endure it, and so provide you with a way out.
> —I CORINTHIANS 10:13

The abbot loses the argument. Shortly thereafter he is alone in his chapel when a final bomb falls and the building collapses on him. Pinned from the waist down by tons of rock, he runs his argument by himself, willing himself consciously to accept his pain, comprehending it and enduring it. He tries another tack of his argument, though no one is left to listen to him:

Why don't you forgive God for allowing pain? If He didn't allow it, human courage, bravery, nobility, and self-sacrifice would all be meaningless things.

Funny thing about physical pain. Once it's over, one cannot recall it. One can remember that one was *in* pain but one cannot *feel* past pain in present comfort. Remembered laughter and happy times can bring a present smile to one's lips; past pain stays there in the past — physical pain, that is. However, the ongoing psychic pain that we suffer over life's losses and deprivations seems to have no end, no relief in sight.

Even after all these years, we can still ask "Why me?" We still seek to understand the meaning of such pain. These haunting, nagging questions sent me back to *Leibowitz* to find that abbot's answer. If there were no pain, then *human courage, bravery, nobility, and self-sacrifice would be meaningless.*

Viktor Frankl warns us that we should not search for an abstract meaning of life. We must be specific, be concrete, be present. I remember writing in my journal when I was first foundering in these questions, "At least I am *present* at my life. I am conscious and present." I thought that was important. I was present and I wasn't going to leave. And then I realized that I wasn't the only one asking questions. We all ask those big ones:

— Why me?
— Where am I going?
— Who am I?
— What have I done to deserve this?

That is, we think we're asking. We have to realize that it's really life that is asking us. Are we ready for the questions? I guess no one ever is.

So what *are* we going to do? Next, I mean. Well, we could stand up, take a big breath, smile, look around, and ask the angel for the blessing. By so doing, we go back to the point of wounding. The angel's flaming sword must exactly fit and cauterize the wound. Then we must go back to the last time we were truly whole — early childhood, maybe — before we gave up so much of our selves to others, to our father, mother, lovers, mates, children, and find all our lost bits and pieces, and put them all together again. This is the *reintegration* that Peter Marris talks about.

I've been thinking hard about that self we have to recover. The trick is to recognize it because it might be different, that is, changed. I've been listening to people's voices as they expressed their thoughts on grieving, and to my own voice. I think I have a clue.

My accountant tells me that once a year when I come in with my bundle of receipts and papers, ready to face my tax reckoning, my voice is not the same as it is at any other time. It's a little-girl, frightened voice, asking for help, begging forgiveness, seeking absolution. (Others who panic at numbers will recognize the feeling that colors that voice.)

I'll be sixty years old by the time this book is published and I've been thinking about that, too, in connection with my voice. What kind of voice is appropriate to a sixty-year-old? Not that Little Girl Voice. Not the Siren Voice (older women are invisible to men). Not the Mother Voice, though I slip into it now more than the others. What I need now is the Crone Voice.

Crone has had bad press; the *Oxford English Dictionary* defines crone as "a withered, old woman," and it raises an image connected (in men's minds) with death. When she is no longer a sex object or child-bearer, an older woman is not allowed to be matriarch because we don't live in a matriarchal society. At least she is no longer murdered as a witch, but she is effectively eliminated (financially, socially) in present-day society. Barbara Walker, in her book *The Crone*, presents another image of crone — as "woman of age, wisdom, and power." That's the voice I want to cultivate. Not Crone, I guess, but Woman — Eternal Woman?

In all fairness, men don't have it easy, either. Their voices are Boy Scout, Man About Town, and Patriarch. At least Patriarch gets to sit on the board and make a few decisions.

What we both have to find, male and female alike, is an authentic voice. After death has wiped away all our easy assumptions about our lives and asked all the hard questions we never wanted to answer, we have to find a way to talk back. We have the tools. I have discussed them and illustrated their use in the recovery of self. It is possible to find a new role and to discover our assignment. We have to come to terms with suffering, and acknowledge the strength that our weakness can give us. The burden is another source of strength and light if it is tackled with guts and grace. The choice is ours. What we are aiming for is the ultimate reintegration, having something to say and the voice to express it.

And then, as if that wasn't enough work, after all that, we have to learn how to let go — again. I knew it was going to be hard but I never knew it was going to be this hard. I think that's the most difficult lesson of all — learning how to let go. I have learned (the hard way) that it's the only way to stay open. If we close in with our loss we'll never be healed. As Scott Peck says in *The Road Less Traveled*,

> *The healing of the spirit has not been completed until openness to challenge becomes a way of life.*

So we must learn to love with open hands. That way the pain slips through our fingers. If we hang on too tightly, we lose everything. But, if we let go and lose everything, we might, just might, regain our self — and a new voice? I hope so. We stand here on the cutting edge of creation. We hold our grief with open hands, offering it as a meaningful sacrifice with, finally, some sense of who we are and what we are doing. We pray — to whomever it is comfortable for us to pray — with a new, confident voice. We might even create our selves.

That's one way.

I thought that was my conclusion, but I was talking to an old friend who helped and hurt me (nothing is ever simple) when I was first widowed. He himself has suffered an unbearable loss, the death of a son in a car accident. He asked what my new book was about and I told him.

"Don't you ever leave it?" he asked.

I wanted to say, "You don't understand," but I didn't because he probably does. Instead I said, "It's not a book I've written before."

But he made me realize how insular I've become: scarred and shielded from pain, cocooned in solitude, protected and maybe even too invulnerable now. I never meant to be like that. Tell me I'm wrong. Tell me another way. I guarantee I'll listen.

Grieving is a continuing, creative process.

Bibliography

Ariès, Philippe. *Centuries of Childhood*. tr. by Robert Baldick. New York: Vintage Books (Random House), 1962

————. *The Hour of Our Death*. tr. by Helen Weaver. New York: Alfred A. Knopf, 1981

Becker, Ernest. *The Denial of Death*. New York: The Free Press, Collier Macmillan, 1973

Bernard, Jessie. *The Future of Marriage*. New Haven and London: Yale University Press, 1982

Bettelheim, Bruno. *Surviving and Other Essays*. New York: Alfred A. Knopf, 1979

Bouvard, Marguerite, in collaboration with Evelyn Gladu. *The Path through Grief*. Portland, Oregon: Breitenbush Books Inc., 1988

Bowlby, John. *Attachment*. New York: Basic Books, Inc., 1969

————. *Separation*. New York: Basic Books, Inc., 1973

————. *Loss*. New York: Basic Books, Inc., 1980

Brett, Simon, ed. *The Faber Book of Diaries*. London: Faber & Faber, 1987

Buck, Pearl. *A Bridge for Passing*. New York: Harper & Row, 1962.

Buckman, Dr. Robert. *I Don't Know What to Say*. Toronto: Key Porter Books, 1988

Caine, Lynn. *Widow*. New York: Bantam Books, 1974

Callwood, June. *Jim: A Life with AIDS*. Toronto: Lester & Orpen Dennys, 1988

————. *Twelve Weeks in Spring*. Toronto: Lester & Orpen Dennys, 1986.

Campbell, Scott, and Phyllis Silverman. *Widower*. New York: Prentice Hall, 1987

Cohen, Donna, and Carl Eisdorfer. *The Loss of Self*. Markham, Ontario: New American Library, Penguin Books, 1986

Comfort, Alex. *A Good Age*. New York: Simon & Schuster, 1976

Culley, Margo, ed. *A Day at a Time*. New York: The Feminist Press, 1985

Deits, Bob. *Life After Loss*. Tucson: Fisher Books, 1988

Dinnerstein, Dorothy. *The Mermaid and the Minotaur*. New York: Harper Colophon Books, 1977

Dohaney, M.T. *When Things Get Back to Normal*. Porters Lake, Nova Scotia: Pottersfield Press, 1989

Dowling, Colette. *The Cinderella Complex*. New York: Pocket Books, 1982

Dustin, Virginia Sheeley. "Just As You Are," *Good Housekeeping*, March 1989

Elmer, Lon. *Why Her Why Now*. New York/Toronto: Bantam Books, 1987

Frankl, Viktor E. *Man's Search for Meaning*. tr. by Ilse Lasch. New York: Simon & Schuster, 1959

Gibran, Kahlil. *The Prophet*. New York: Alfred A. Knopf, 1923

Gilligan, Carol. *In a Different Voice*. Cambridge, Mass.: Harvard University Press, 1983

Griffiths, Linda. "Prayer Before an Abortion," from *The Darling Family*, *Prairie Journal of Canadian Literature*, No. 12, 1989–90

Grollman, Earl. Speech delivered to the Bereaved Families of Ontario, Ottawa chapter, May 1990

Gunther, John. *Death Be Not Proud*. New York: Harper & Row, 1949

Hartman, Linda. *The Day After Death*.

Holmes, T.H., and R.H. Rahe. "The Social Adjustment Rating Scale." *Journal of Psychosomatic Research* 11 (1967): 213–18.

Ibsen, Henrik. *Brand*. tr. F.E. Garrett. London: J.M. Dent & Son, 1915

Johnstone, Keith. *Impro*. London: Faber & Faber, 1979

Kübler-Ross, Elisabeth. *Death: The Final Stage of Growth*. New York: Simon & Schuster, 1986

————. *Living with Death and Dying*. New York: Collier Macmillan, 1981

————. *Questions and Answers on Death and Dying*. New York: Collier Macmillan, 1974

————. *AIDS: The Ultimate Challenge*. New York: Collier Macmillan, 1989

Kushner, Harold. *When Bad Things Happen to Good People*. New York: Schocken Books, 1981

Lukas, Christopher, and Henry M. Seiden. *Silent Grief: Living in the Wake of Suicide*. New York: Bantam Books, 1990

Lerner, Harriet Goldhor. *The Dance of Anger*. New York: Harper & Row, 1985

Lewis, C.S. *A Grief Observed*. London: Faber & Faber, 1961

————. *The Problem of Pain*. London: Fontana Books, Collins, 1957

Lifton, Robert Jay, and Eric Olson. *Living and Dying*. New York: Bantam Books, 1974

Luria, A.R. *The Neuropsychology of Memory*, quoted in *The Man Who Mistook His Wife for a Hat* by Oliver Sacks

Linn, Erin. *150 Facts about Grieving Children*. Nevada: The Publisher's Mark, 1990

Marris, Peter. *Loss and Change*. Garden City, New York: Anchor Books, Doubleday, 1975

Maxwell, William. *So Long, See You Tomorrow*. Originally appeared in *The New Yorker*. c. 1979

Millay, Edna St. Vincent. "Dirge Without Music" from *Collected Poems*. New York: Harper & Row, 1928

Miller, Jean Baker. *Toward a New Psychology of Women*. Boston: Beacon Press, 1986

Miller, Walter M. *A Canticle for Leibowitz*. New York: Bantam Books, 1988

Moffatt, Betty Clare. *When Someone You Love Has AIDS*. New York, Scarborough: NAL Penguin, 1986

Moffatt, Mary Jane. *In the Midst of Winter: Selections from the Literature of Mourning*. New York: Vintage Books, Random House, 1982

Monette, Paul. *Borrowed Time*. New York: Avon Books, 1988

Munro, Alice. *Friend of My Youth*. Toronto: McClelland & Stewart, 1990

Myers, Gerald E. *Self: An Introduction to Philosophical Psychology*. New York: Pegasus, 1969

O'Connor, Elizabeth. *Journey Inward, Journey Outward.* New York, Harper & Row, 1975

Oliver, Rose, and Frances A. Bock. *Coping with Alzheimer's*. California: Wilshire Book Company, 1987

Ornstein, Robert, and David Sobel. *The Healing Brain*. New York: Simon & Schuster, 1987

Page, Louise. "Tissue" in *Plays by Women*, Volume One. edited by Micheline Wandor. London: Methuen, 1982.

Peck, M. Scott. *The Road Less Traveled*. New York: Simon & Schuster, 1978.

Perrot, Michelle, ed. *A History of Private Life,* Vol. IV. tr. Arthur Goldhammer. Cambridge, Mass.: Belknap Press, 1990

Philipe, Anne. *No Longer Than a Sigh*. tr. Cornelia Schaeffer. New York: Atheneum Publishers, 1964

Pincus, Lily. *Death and the Family*. New York: Vintage Books, Random House, 1974

Ross, Marvin. *The Silent Epidemic* (Alzheimer's). Willowdale, Ont.: Hounslow Press, 1987

Sacks, Oliver. *The Man Who Mistook His Wife for a Hat*. New York: Summit Books, 1985

Schiff, Harriet Sarnoff. *The Bereaved Parent*. New York: Penguin Books, 1977

Schreiber, Le Anne. *Midstream: The Story of a Mother's Death and a Daughter's Renewal*. New York: Viking, Penguin, 1990

Schwartz, Mimi. "Living with Loss, Dreaming of Lace," *Lear's* magazine, October 1990

Selye, Hans. *The Stress of Life*. New York: McGraw-Hill, 1956

Shain, Merle. *Some Men Are More Perfect than Others*. Toronto: Bantam Books, 1974

Shaw, G.B. *The Doctors' Dilemma*. Harmondsworth: Penguin Books, 1946

Shorter, Edward. *The Making of the Modern Family*. New York: Basic Books, 1977

Silverman, William B., and Kenneth M. Cinnamon. *When Mourning Comes*. Chicago: Nelson-Hall, 1982

Sontag, Susan. *Illness as Metaphor*. New York: Farrar, Straus and Giroux, 1978

Stanton, Steve. "Certificate in Escrow," *Prairie Journal of Canadian Literature*, No. 12, 1989–90

Stearns, Ann Kaiser. *Living through Personal Crisis*. New York: Ballantine Books, 1984

Steinfels, Peter, and Robert M. Veatch, eds. *Death Inside Out*. New York: Harper & Row, 1975

Stock, Gregory. *The Book of Questions*. New York: Workman Publishing, 1987

Swift, Jonathan. *Gulliver's Travels*. New York: Viking Press, 1948.

Storr, Anthony. *Solitude: A Return to the Self*. New York: Ballantine Books, 1988

Talbot, Toby. *A Book about My Mother*. New York: Farrar, Straus and Giroux, 1980

Thomas, Dylan. "Do Not Go Gentle . . ." from *Collected Works*. London: J.M. Dent & Son

Toffler, Alvin. *Future Shock*. New York: Bantam Books, 1980

Viorst, Judith. *Necessary Losses*. New York: Simon & Schuster, 1986

Wells, Rosemary. *Helping Children Cope with Grief*. London: Sheldon Press, 1988

West, Paul. *Words for a Deaf Daughter*. New York: Harper & Row, 1970.

Westberg, Granger E. *Good Grief*. Philadelphia: Fortress Press, 1989

Woodman, Marion. *Addiction to Perfection*. Toronto: Inner City Books, 1982

Woolf, Virginia. *A Room of One's Own*. New York: Harcourt Brace Jovanovich, 1929

Wylie, Betty Jane. *Beginnings: A Book for Widows*. Toronto: McClelland & Stewart, 1988

———. *The Book of Matthew*. Toronto: McClelland & Stewart, 1985

———. *Successfully Single*. Toronto: Key Porter Books, 1987

———. *Something Might Happen*. Windsor: Black Moss Press, 1989

———. *The Old Woman and the Pedlar*. Toronto: Playwrights Press, 1978.

Yates, Martha. *Coping, A Survival Manual for Women Alone*. New Jersey: Prentice-Hall, 1976

Resources

A Beginning, one of the books in a kit for recently bereaved parents of infants, can be purchased separately by mail. Write: Women's College Hospital, 76 Grenville St., Toronto, Ontario M5S 1B2. And ask about the booklet *Healing a Father's Grief*.

The *Newsletter* of the Elisabeth Kübler-Ross Center publishes useful information about books, videos, and tapes for all ages encountering grief, as well as addresses of networking and support groups. Write: The Elisabeth Kübler-Ross Center, South Rte. 616, Head Waters, Virginia, USA 24442

I am intrigued by one booklet mentioned in the newsletter sample I received. It's called *Write Grief: How To Transform Loss with Writing*, by Gail B. Jacobsen, available for $4.95 (US) plus $1.50 shipping from McCormick and Schilling, P.O. Box 722, Menomonee Falls, Wisconsin, USA 53051.

Another quarterly newsletter, *Caring Concepts*, comes with a membership in Centering Corporation, Box 3367, Omaha, Nebraska, USA 68103.

Here's a Canadian resource: *Initiative*, The Self-Help Newsletter, Canadian Council on Social Development, Box 3505, Station C, 56 Parkdale, Ottawa, Ontario K1Y 4G1. The sample copy I have includes tips for Alzheimer's caregivers, a report of cancer patients' self-help groups, a calendar of events (support groups) across Canada, and a list of resources.

To find out more about the Living Will, write: Dying with Dignity, 175 St. Clair Ave. W., Toronto, Ontario M4V 1P7

I also recommend: *The Journal of Palliative Care*, 30 Prince Arthur Ave., Toronto, Ontario M5R 1B2

Index